Old Enough to Know Better

ALSO BY PAUL ST. PIERRE

Boss of the Namko Drive

Breaking Smith's Quarter Horse

Chilcotin Holiday

Sister Balonika

British Columbia: Our Land

Smith and Other Events: Stories of the Chilcotin

Chilcotin and Beyond

In the Navel of the Moon

Tell Me a Good Lie: Tales from the Chilcotin Country

Old Enough to Know Better

PAUL ST PIERRE

HARBOUR PUBLISHING

Copyright © 2002 Paul St. Pierre

All rights reserved. No part of this publication may be reproduced, stored in a retrieval system or transmitted, in any form or by any means, without prior permission of the publisher or, in the case of photocopying or other reprographic copying, a licence from CANCOPY (Canadian Reprography Collective), 214 King Street West, Toronto, Ontario, M5H 3S6

Published by
Harbour Publishing
P.O. Box 219, Madeira Park,
BC Canada
V0N 2H0

www.harbourpublishing.com

Printed in Canada.

Design by Martin Nichols
Editing by Naomi Pauls
Cover illustration by Peter Lynde

We acknowledge the financial support of the Government of Canada through the Book Publishing Industry Development Program for our publishing activities. We further acknowledge the support of the Canada Council for the Arts and the Province of British Columbia through the British Columbia Arts Council for our publishing program.

THE CANADA COUNCIL | LE CONSEIL DES ARTS
FOR THE ARTS | DU CANADA
SINCE 1957 | DEPUIS 1957

National Library of Canada Cataloguing in Publication Data

St. Pierre, Paul, 1923–
   Old enough to know better

   ISBN 1-55017-276-X

   I. Title.
PS8537.A54O42 2002   C814'.54   C2002-910759-8
PR9199.3.S16O42 2002

*To the St. Pierre family,
which flourishes like the green bay tree*

Contents

Introduction 9

Social Swings and Roundabouts
Throw Him in Backup, She's All Spoil 15
Utopia, My Favourite Girlfriend 26
Message? What Message? 33
Sex, Marriage, Sweet Women and All That Sort of Thing 42
There Is Life After Television 63
The Vile Brute Within 67
Time Surprises Old Father William 73
The Secrets of Success 80

Verities and Mysteries
Faith in Fuzzy Quantums 89
The Mad, Glad Impulse 97
Secrets, Codes, Computers and Cover-ass 104
Ye Gods! 113
Circles, Cubes and Luscious Rot 126
Art Outlives Us 132
Who Is That Mysterious Masked Stranger? It's You 135

How to Run the Country
Henry Ford Freed Us, the Rulers Retaliated 145
Who Really Runs the Country? 152
How We MPs Saved the Lemmings 161
Judges Are from Mars 184
Common Man's Best Friend: A King or Queen 192
The Law and the Reality 200
Fascism, an Idea Whose Time Has Come 204
Pretend You Paid for This Advice 213

Wisdoms Gone Old and Stale
Beware the Righteous Man 231
The Seven Sins Aren't So Deadly 234
The Truth About Lying 236
In Trust We Trust 239
Intellectuals Have Meagre Souls 243
How to Tell Sheepshit from Boston Baked Beans 246
Joy 249
Conclusion 250

Acknowledgements 254

Introduction

WHEN I WAS GROWING UP and the family were trying to civilize me the adults would say, when I did something unusually wild or foolish, that I was old enough to know better. It was a phrase I learned to detest. I was almost always old enough to know better than to enjoy what I was doing.

We keep hearing this said all our lives. Women of 40 who have a sexual encounter with a man of 20 are told they are old enough to know better. Psychologists who study men in their Foolish Fifties say the male has a natural impulse to seek romance at that age. Usually he seeks it with a female half his age, but some men fall in love with their own wives a second time. It's a yearning for hearts and flowers, and everybody agrees that they are old enough to know better.

Is there never a point in our lives at which the phrase becomes positive instead of negative? Isn't there some time when we *do* know better than other people, including our critics? As a matter of fact, yes. I am at that age. I know a hell of a lot better about things than most of you and I know immensely more than I did a mere ten years ago. What is perhaps most important of all, I have discovered brand-new questions—questions I thought were answered to my satisfaction decades and decades ago. Suddenly, there they are again, unanswered and by me unanswerable.

I grew old enough to know better after three score years and ten. I am now eight years past the mark set by the Christians as the birthday when we should cash in our chips and quit the game so younger people can get to the table. I have news for the Christians and for the younger people. I have no intention of going. But what the hell, to borrow another Christian expression, death is going to happen whether I want it to or not and, as I suggest in one of the chapters in this book, perhaps it should come regularly at age 70. Possibly our society should arrange farewell euthanasia banquets for our seventieth birthdays, but meantime I take the highly personal if selfish view that I should remain alive, indefinitely.

I write this book for descendants I shall never see but also for myself. Here are set out the truths that eluded me when I was a kid under 70 and the questions I should have been asking. They are conclusions reached without my consciously seeking them, still less processing them with logical thought. One of the things I have learned is that logic has little to do with how human beings behave and that we are often happier and have a lot more fun when not trying to invoke it. Perhaps what has interested me most and which I trust will interest my great-grandchildren, if they can read once they reach adulthood, is that in my seventies some of the supposedly eternal verities that had been central to my life have suddenly become shifty, uncertain and unsure.

Critics may say that I am a person who might be wrong but is never in doubt. I try to be that way. How can I be sure of the truths that have become apparent to me, or the occasional doubts, for that matter? Go ahead, ask, but ask somebody else, not me. I don't know. I do know that what I write here is highly personal, sometimes cranky I suppose, and possibly wrong-headed. I don't much care. I also feel under no obligation to be fair to those of opposing views, a great burden to have lifted from one's shoulders after a lifetime working in newspapers.

These are also the expressions of a heterosexual male, because that is what I am. Here you will not find me pleading the cause of females or homosexuals, both of whom are noisy enough that the world can hear their message loud and clear. I mention sex because, being a member of the provably weaker sex, there is a curl in my mind that cannot be ironed flat. The best comparison is the domestic dog. As those who have made pets of wolves will understand, and many have made pets of wolves, the wolf becomes an adult and an associate rather than a pet. The domestic dog is far different. He never grows up. He remains a child from birth to death. So, in many respects, does the human male. He is emotional, filled with foolish notions, wild impulses; he chases his own tail, he has fun, he has joy, he has wild and foolish dreams. As with dogs, it makes us lovable.

This is also written as a Canadian. Apparently I am also an American. I don't know (and never made the effort to find out), but I do know I am Canadian, because when Americans are calling something super sensational, marvellous, absolutely fabulous, I always call it not bad. That is a good way to tell a Canadian from an American.

Readers will notice, I hope, that Goodthink and Newspeak do not appear on these pages. The chattering classes call chairmen *chairs* now but I am still more at ease with real English language as found in the *Oxford English Dictionary*, and were I writing an adventure story, my captain would not shout "Person the lifeboats!" nor would the crewmen cry out "Persons and children first into the boats!"

In ending this introduction, I offer an apology. Despite more than a third of a century trying to keep the word out of my newspaper columns, in this book the ugly word *I* speckles every page like flies on a cowflap. This person regrets that.

Social Swings and Roundabouts

Throw Him in Backup, She's All Spoil

I caming old country five years long. Today I talking the England good as for you and twice as more.
— Ukrainian immigrant studying English

NOW AND THEN A TELEVISION INTERVIEWER, who himself may count barely fifty-two cards in his deck, will ask the ultimate foolish question of a visiting politician. "If you could have anything you wish, what would it be?" Being a silly question, it gets a silly answer. The politician says he would ask for a world where wars were no more and poverty and hunger and racial prejudice had been banned from the face of the earth. Did the interviewer anticipate he might come out strongly in favour of war, poverty, disease and covering blacks with diesel oil and burning them in the town square? A Boston Pizza ad is more intellectually stimulating than this humbug.

Yet a similar question could be put, which would deserve a reasonable answer. "You have one wish to be granted. Speaking as a practical man, what would you want to see done to make our society better?" There's a question with the soapsuds squeezed out. It can be picked up and handled.

I have a wish. Mine would be for restoration of the English language, which has been damn near destroyed by the people on what we foolishly refer to as the cutting edge of society. English only, I say. The French speakers, the Basques, the Norwegians and the Vietnamese have spoiled their languages also, but they will have to speak for themselves. I speak for the only language I know well, English, a noble instrument when properly used.

Two examples of the spoliation of English are at my hand. One is stored in memory, because it is easy to remember, and the other is on paper to be read because few people could memorize it or would want to.

I snitched the second from a bulletin board in my daughter's high school, some years ago. The Grade Eights were raising hell, as Grade Eights often do, and the teacher who wrote the note was calling a meeting to see what could be done about the little bastards, I think. Here is how he expressed himself in Shakespeare's tongue:

"The purpose of the meeting is to collaboratively define or establish designed experience for the Grade 8ers. That is, all of his/her experiences in the halls, the grounds and the classrooms are part of an intentional interface—no laissez faire. One parameter is to embrace diversity while inculcating the integrity of our purpose." That writer probably has a university degree.

The other document was a pencilled note, stuck under my door by a handyman. "weNt to STOAR for hinjEs they aint Got none rite sizes." This man probably did not complete Grade 4.

Both of these men are almost illiterate, one because he has too little formal education and the other because he has too much. As to which of them can best use English, the handyman wins, easily. He knows that the purpose of a language is to transmit thoughts and information from one person to another. It is almost the only purpose of spoken or written words.

(There are exceptions. A mother, crooning a lullaby to a baby who knows none of the words and couldn't understand them even if they made sense, may use words that make no sense whatever. In this case it doesn't matter. She is not trying to convey meaning; she wants to convey a feeling of love and security to the infant. She acts instinctively in the same way that, eight times out of ten, she will cradle her baby in her left arm so that her warm and meaningless words enter the baby's left ear and go directly to the right hemisphere of the brain, which is the intuitive side and which in children develops faster than the left hemisphere.)

However, meaningless English from a semi-literate schoolteacher has no such redeeming qualities. He should be using English to communicate facts. He either cannot or will not. We can only guess at what he is saying. We can't even be sure he is trying to say anything.

Why, then, is he committing these indecent acts upon English in public? There are several possible explanations, and none of them is pleasant to think about.

He may have been educated beyond his intelligence and believe there is something suspect, perhaps degrading, in speaking simply and clearly. He may not be able to think simply and clearly and the murky cloud of words and near words reflects the state of his mind. He may realize that thinking is not what he is good at and for that reason devises the pompous gitch to hide that weakness. He may feel that although the world in general will not understand him his fellow professionals will, and that is what matters. He and they speak a special language to one another; it excludes the great unwashed multitudes of the public. This explanation raises the horrid thought that all the teachers of the school are as illiterate as he is.

The probable explanation is that all these forces are at work in varying degrees—an education system that has failed to teach simple, declarative prose; a small mind made timid by a world where other people seem to be so much more knowledgeable; a conviction that long words are always better than short ones and that four words are as much better than three as three are better than two. He would be puzzled, almost alarmed, by the dictum of Winston Churchill: "Short words are best and the old words when short are best of all." What Mr. Churchill would have said about the schoolteacher's memo we can never know but we can guess. When he encountered a message from a civil servant in which a sentence had been stood on its head so that it would not end with a preposition, Mr. Churchill wrote, "This is the sort of English up with which I will not put."

Why should a British prime minister heed so small a matter and why should I care about jargon in the classroom? There are other problems in this world that are large and ferocious: cancer, the decline of the world's fisheries, the AIDS epidemic, wars and rumours of war. I say only that languages are the stems on which men all over the world develop their intellect. Recent discoveries indicate that language is central to brain development. I call as witness Otto von Bismarck, who said the most important event in world history was that English, instead of Dutch, French or Spanish, became the language of America.

Alas, some of today's political leaders don't share Mr. Bismarck's view.

There have been a couple of American presidents who could not handle English. The first George Bush was one. An admirable man, Mr. Bush. Any man who makes his first parachute jump at age 75 just for the sport of it is admirable. But when he started a sentence he had great difficulty remembering what he set out to say as he ambled through it. When he got to the end he wasn't quite sure what it was he had started out to say, except that there had been a fuzzy warmth to it that made him feel good.

H.L. Mencken, making much the same criticism of President W.G. Harding, said that that president's English was so bad that a sort of grandeur crept into it.

Forget parachute jumping, forget Mencken's wit: in international affairs this inability to arrange and project one's thoughts in the native language is a risky business. People can get hurt while experts are submitting presidential statements to torture, hoping they will yield up their meaning.

Most of us recognize the danger of misunderstanding when languages are translated from one to another. The argument is made that the Japanese, whose language is notorious for its circumlocution, thought they were making an offer of surrender before the bombs fell on Hiroshima and Nagasaki but did so in cloudy language. Had they spoken clearly, a quarter of a million civilian lives might have been spared.

When the confusion exists in the mouth and mind of our own people, speaking our own language to us, there's a serious problem, with which we have not grappled. It is a problem and also a symptom. When we choose bloated, pompous twaddle instead of plain old Anglo-Saxon noun-verb-object sentences, we say something about the state of ourselves and our view of society.

Yes, there is a human tendency to cover hard facts with soft words. I took a boy out fishing once whose father had just died. What else can you do for a kid who has just lost his best friend? All day the boy kept circling the word *dead*. "My father, before he expired..." "This was before my father's demise..." "My father, who has passed away..." "My dad, whose life has terminated..." I was tempted to say, "Tom, your dad is dead, dead, dead," but such things are never said to the grieving, even though they should be said to newspaper editors, and even I, when forced into that most unhappy task of notifying somebody of a death in the family, have invariably retreated to the euphemism "passed away." But the jargoneer does not speak muddily because he is interested in sparing the feelings of other people. Almost invariably he is fascinated with himself to the exclusion of all else. That and concealing instead of revealing meanings.

In war, our army's defeats are customarily announced in language designed to take people's minds off what is being said to them. This makes exceptions so exhilarating and, at times, inspiring. Again, we turn to Churchill, speaking in the British House of Commons: "The news from France is very bad."

Edwin Newman wrote two excellent books about the abuse of English, *Strictly Speaking* and *A Civil Tongue*. They soared to the top of the *New York Times* best-seller list, as so many good and bad books do, and in a short time disappeared without trace. There was one reprint of the two combined, *Edwin Newman on Language*, issued in 1980. It, too, is now out of print and all the books are collector's items. These books were worth a dozen chairs of literature at Yale, Harvard, McGill and other universities, and their burial is little short of tragedy for the people of the English-speaking world. However, we brought it on ourselves. We didn't buy enough of them.

Meanwhile the barbarians are raping and pillaging English. As with the Gauls, the Vandals and the Huns, some of the roving wrecking gangs are worse than others. Academics are among the worst offenders, as our sample above indicates. There are far worse listed in Mr. Newman's books.

Another wantonly destructive group are the sociologists. *New York Times* columnist Russell Baker credited them with inventing a brand-new language, the only language ever born dead.

Army generals aspiring to greater futilities seem to believe that absurd English is the road to promotion, and call targets "preselected impact areas."

Simple old political lying invites the cloudy cover of jargon. When President Nixon lied one day his spokesman next morning fixed everything by saying that the president's answer the day before was "no longer operative."

Sportscasters are another group—"a genuine human being in his own right"—but perhaps they don't matter because we expect them to drag their knuckles on the ground and gibber. Also, let it be admitted, the trade was a successful apprenticeship for some superb writers. The other jargon speakers have much to answer for, if not in this life then in the next, because while an increasingly complicated society requires clear communication, they lead in the opposite direction, making the simple complicated, making the short and simple long and tortuous, and making all things worse by being pompous, silly and stupid. Their speech and writing warps English at all levels of society.

Today scarcely anybody can bear to use the word *important*, which means important. The word *importantly* is substituted because it has four syllables instead of three. The word *importantly* does not mean important, it means pompously or stuffily, but presently we seem to have agreed to pretend otherwise. Note please the word *presently*. Because it is longer and has three syllables we use it instead of *now*, which has only one. It is not used accurately. Presently does not mean at present, it means soon. People who say presently also lift their little finger to the sky when they sip a cup of tea.

I take no such offence at bad spelling. Spelling doesn't matter much. By accident of birth as much as anything, I am a rather good speller, but I never believed the talent amounted to much, particularly in the English language, where spelling is so often remote from pronunciation. Punctilious spelling is recent anyway. The Elizabethans were still spelling their words, as best they could, phonetically, and one of them, Shakespeare, wasn't even consistent in spelling his own name.

Nor would I ever condemn slang. I am more apt to welcome it. Slang is used by real people, often saying real things. Slang is sometimes lazy shortcut talk, but it is not sleazy and it is often witty, clever and deserves entry into the dictionaries. When somebody says, "Pass me the young hammer," I know he means the smaller one and a tedious job is made easier by such small alterations of phraseology. The same may be said of fractured English. I think of the example of the Indian from Chilcotin, speaking English as a second language, a late second language, telling about having his truck transmission spit up teeth into his lap. People speak of the language he uses to describe his plight as unconscious humour. Little humour is. Unconscious humour is about as rare as extemporaneous political remarks. The Indian knows his knowledge of English is poor but he wants to arrange the few words he has so they entertain as well as inform. He is from a verbal society where clever use of words is appreciated and he is going to try it in a foreign language. Look how well he does:

"Goin' down Sheep Creek Hill. Brakes them don't work. Throw him in backup, she's aaaaaall spoil." Crude and memorable, as is also the man on the bucking horse who reported, "My hat goes off both sides of the road. I'm a one-man crowd."

All this is to speak only of utilitarian English, the use of words to carry information among us and, quite often, to crystallize our own thoughts that had been hitherto random and disorganized.

Beyond the crying need for clear speech is another quality. Beauty. It can never be given to everyone to create beautiful English because that is magic and magic, like friendship, like humour, lies beyond the reach of explanation. Some people seem to be born to spasms of the magic and even in translation from one language to another they do not lose it. There is no better example than the author (believed to be Solomon) of Ecclesiastes. Consider the magic of this well-known passage: "I returned, and saw under the sun, that the race is not to the swift, nor the battle to the strong, neither yet bread to the wise, nor yet riches to men of understanding, nor yet favour to men of skill; but time and chance happeneth to them all." It moves the soul.

Interestingly enough, it is not good English, any more than my handyman's semi-literate note is good English. Time happeneth? Time cannot happen. Like depth, width and breadth, it is a dimension of what is called space-time and cannot happen any more than length can be said to happen. Such a quibble amounts to nothing in the face of magic English, which for all its many borrowings is essentially the Anglo-Saxon tongue, and at its most powerful and moving when it is slightly inaccurate. For hundreds of years, millions of Christians, most of whom could not read or write during several of those centuries, have had no difficulty in understanding Ecclesiastes' words, the beauty of which seized and held their imaginations.

Abraham Lincoln: "Four score and seven years ago our forefathers brought forth on this continent a new nation, conceived in Liberty and dedicated to the proposition that all men are created equal." All wrong. If he meant eighty-seven years, why didn't he say eighty-seven? But we know it is not all wrong, it is all right, because of the magic.

Consider how much is said, with beauty, on an old rancher's gravestone. "Ray Thomson. He rode good horses and he loved this country."

Or on Judge Begbie's: "Lord, Have Mercy on Me, a Sinner."

Or John Donne: "Come live with me, and be my love, / And we will some new pleasures prove / Of golden sands, and crystal brooks / With silken lines, and silver hooks."

Too ornate? Try simpler.

"There once was a woman, beautiful as the morning..."

Or "Jesus wept."

We usually find the best language in our past, because time has a way of sorting out the great from the near great. (Separation from the trash is, of course, fairly easy.) That words and phrases last over the decades and centuries is their triumph. And yet we are in dire peril if we look only into our past for great English.

The language must grow. If we attempt to freeze it in its present form, as the French Academy does with their language, we may find that English joins French as a declining force in world affairs. So far English continues to spread. It is the new Latin of the business and industrial world and, increasingly, the diplomatic world. French is more suitable for diplomacy because of its use of the conditional verb, which we rather foolishly abandoned. However, the sheer force of English has reversed the tradition of hundreds of years that international affairs are best conducted in French. We leave the French language in possession of fine cookery, where the English can make no claim whatsoever.

The growing force of English is due in part to the fact that English speakers have traditionally not been afraid to borrow from other tongues and to invent their own new words. Shakespeare, one man, added several hundred words to the English language. The French Academy, with a fortress mentality, merely attempts to exclude borrowings from other languages by diktat. Those academicians should remember Napoleon's dictum: "The army which remains behind fortified positions will always be defeated."

There is the difference: on one side, a vigorous and growing language experimenting with new words and borrowing others from the neighbours, on the other a language where society's small-minded people try to make themselves seem important by using impenetrable speech. If you can't see that difference, to hell with you, I have wasted a lot of words on this chapter.

If you think I speak as an English expert, you haven't been paying enough attention. I am not an English expert, I am an English lover. Like any lover, I am often at a loss to understand the one loved—soon, no doubt, to be called the lovee.

Even apart from the occasional occurrence of magic, there are many factors beyond my understanding. The word *shit*, for example. It is not a polite word. *Excrement* is acceptable. Shit comes from the Anglo-Saxon, excrement from the French brought to England by William the Conqueror's Normans. They mean the same thing, not something similar—something exactly the same. There is no shade of difference in the meaning of those two words. The origin of the duality is clear. In the time of the Norman ascendancy in England, using excrement identified you as a member of the ruling class and using shit meant you were a contemptible Anglo-Saxon villein.

How can ancient snobbery remain imbedded in a language for nine hundred years? I don't know. I repeat, I don't know much about English.

As for perfection, English and all the other languages will never make much more than a general approach to that condition. For all that we love the sound and treasure the thoughts that spoken and written language can inspire, we are still but a few, short steps beyond grunting and rubbing the belly to say "I am hungry."

The most exquisite passages of English convey things subtly different to different people. As for the law, where we painstakingly attempt to make every word precise and utterly comprehensible, the meaning of words is disputed daily in every court of the land, and frequently a court composed of our most brilliant judges can only attempt to define a meaning by rendering a majority vote.

All this about English has been written with inadequate understanding but with good intentions to do harm to the wrecking gang. I shall feel rewarded if I do no more than bruise the shins of a few of the puffed up, pompous horse's asses who are misusing English and doing so with the worst will in the world.

As Noel Coward said, they "should be taken out and hung / for the cold-blooded murder of the English tongue." He should have said hanged, but that's English for you.

Utopia, My Favourite Girlfriend

IN THE DAYS WHEN THE EARTH WAS YOUNG, I knew many things that my elders had failed to learn and one of these was the form of the perfect society. It was so obvious, I should have known I was wrong. The obvious is seldom true. My perfect society was anarchy, based on the good old principle that the domination of one human being by another was wrong. All governments were wrong, a violation of nature's law. Jesus was on my side, he talked of the Kingdom of God that would someday replace the kingdoms of men. Karl Marx had the same insight and wrote about the classless, stateless society of the future. To my mind then, governments could be good or bad but even the most benign of them was evil, even if the least of evils.

The facts don't support this vision. There is an immense impulse to collectivism in *Homo sapiens* and collectives must be governed by leaders. The evidence is also more than ample that a large number of human beings prefer to be led than to be leaders. There is equal evidence that leaders are born, not made. There exists in some men and women an impulse to control the people around them, to set their goals, to shape their lives and, usually, to take tax money from them. The goal of the people with the governing instinct may be good, even immaculate, or it may not be, but the act of governing other people fulfills an inner need for many individuals.

This was one of the things most notable to me when I attended the 28th Parliament of Canada. Few, perhaps none of the Members of Parliament in that House were new to political life when they were elected. All whom I had contact with, and that was most of them, argued politics at the family dinner table. They had parents, close relatives and very close friends who were dedicated politicians. Few had a loyalty to any political faith, and a Liberal household could produce a socialist or a conservative as readily as another Liberal. It was not a dedication to party or policy that seemed to be carried in the genes, but a hunger to reshape the lives of people they did not know and might never meet. It is called public service by those who practise it and no doubt it often is.

There was another characteristic of people in Parliament, totally unrelated as far as I can tell, but one that bears mention at this point. Among MPs more than the usual proportion were the lame and the halt. The failure of part or almost all of the body seemed to nourish political growth. I mention this as a curiosity, not as a provable cause of a hunger for the public life but merely as an observable fact.

Of course, it is not only humans who divide themselves into a few leaders and many led. Most wild creatures have the same visible impulse. In the wolf family, a dominant female usually leads the pack—the subject of female leadership is dealt with later in this chapter—and in horses, cattle, sheep and fish the many normally subject themselves to some direction from the few. A place where leaders and followers are most clearly distinguished is in the domestic fowl, and few of nature's creatures have such rotten natures. The pack instinct in fowl leads them to peck weaker members to death, for no reason other than that they perceive it a good idea. Few creatures are less intelligent in their obedience to leadership. The runt of a group, the one lowest in the pecking order, which is pecked by all others but never finds one weaker than itself to peck, may be changed to No. 1 in the pecking order by hormones. When the hormones are removed, it reverts to the poor physical specimen it was in the first place but the rest of the pack are too stupid to notice and the reconstituted runt may continue No. 1 in the order of pecking. People who are disappointed in political leaders they choose might do better had they had more experience in the barnyard.

So, after a few encounters with realities, impelled by the forces of intellect and the even more powerful forces of common sense, I abandoned my plan to make human beings self-sufficient by forcing them into the mould I had made. At about that time I also discovered other activities, such as sex and drinking rum, and utopia faded in importance. Much, much later, when I grew old enough to know better, I returned to the pursuit of the perfect society, this time looking for a pattern suited to man instead of trying to suit man to my pattern. Here it is.

In the ideal society, women would do all the heavy lifting. The females would not only bear the children, do some cooking and provide some sexual excitement, they would also be in charge of all industry, commerce, government and banking, to name a few. This is only fair. They are by far the stronger sex and should be taking on the main work of running a successful society. In a later chapter I deal with this subject of female strength and male weakness in much more detail, including the fact that the male sex may be headed for extinction, leaving behind only a faint, warm racial memory of the swaggering gallantry with which we screwed things up. Suffice it here to mention a few of the qualities that make women fit to run the world.

They have a natural impulse and talent to make different and sometimes antagonistic human beings co-operate with one another for the common good. This is fundamental to family life but equally so the corporate structure, where the management of personalities is usually more important than the mere matter of producing pop-up toasters a little faster and cheaper. The best executives are those who can build teamwork. That happens to be the natural role of the female in humans, as in a pride of lions or a band of wild horses.

As for the nuts-and-bolts work—welding gas pipelines, paving highways or building rocket ships—the Second World War established beyond argument that women could do all these just as well as men. A sole exception is work requiring upper-body muscles, and the reference above to females doing all the heavy lifting should be read as symbolic. They do usually lack upper-body strength and to the intense regret of some of them it keeps them out of the Sandhogs union and the Cape Breton coal mine draegermen teams. However, by the year 2000 there was scarcely a single human quality less in demand than the ability to pack a hundred pounds of potatoes on one's shoulder. Scarcely anybody was paying for muscle power any more. In the few instances where it is still necessary, tomorrow's females can use male servants to perform such tasks.

An argument frequently raised against the presence of women in the boardroom is that they tend to be emotional. Of all the silly arguments raised by males, this must surely be among the most fatuous. Of course women let emotions rule, in almost everything they do in life. That is what is so splendid about them. They know what is important. Emotions, not money, are what our world is all about. As Napoleon said in defending his decision to introduce the Legion of Honour, "Men are led by baubles." He could have uttered this truth in different words by saying men are led by emotions. Anything worth doing in this world brings emotional rather than financial reward. Emotional leadership is what we crave but seldom get, except briefly, during wartime. Any who doubt this should read *Emotional Intelligence*, by Daniel Goleman.

Men have also raised objections to my utopian plan. They say it will make women bossy. Where, exactly, have these males spent their lives up until now? Have they known no females?

I have known my share of females: mother, aunts, nieces, daughters, granddaughters, also two wives and some live-in girlfriends. There has never been one of them who did not, from time to time, as a matter of right and duty, seek to stop me doing things I wanted to do and start me doing things I did not want to do. Power, not Montessori schools or cravings for new shoes, is the primary passion of the human female. They think their purpose in life is to control males, and probably it is. The urge to manipulate is inborn. You may observe this at any riding stable, where teenaged girls show such evident delight in taking a creature that is much larger, stronger and in some respects smarter than they are and, by a series of tricks, rendering it completely subservient to their will. There is nothing wrong with this, any more than there is anything wrong with women having high voices and wide hips. That is how things are. If we had a bit more of the Taoist philosophy on this continent, men might see the virtue of harmonizing themselves with the natural forces of the universe, particularly the natural force called female.

What, then, does remain for men to do in my new society? Plenty, and it will be more attuned to their natures. In this perfect society men will sit around and talk quite a bit. They will write poetry now and then and tell stirring stories to each other. More important, they will tell inspiring stories grown into legends to the children and grandchildren, a precious gift of the ages that has withered in the second half of the twentieth century.

Men will dance, sing, paint and argue philosophy. They will get drunk now and then. From time to time they will arrange a gentlemanly war.

War of course repels many people. Women in particular do not like wars. However, despite that, women serve as a catalyst to promote wars. The arrival of a woman president or prime minister in a nation is usually a prelude to war. Madames Thatcher, Ghandi, Bandaranaike... the list is as long as the fighting is inevitable and began with Helen of Troy.

If left to themselves, however, men would be likely to civilize war again. Professional soldiers only would participate. Civilians would be told they were not good enough and sent to places of safety. Civilians who persisted in taking part in a war would be stoned to death.

Also we could anticipate that never again would the monstrous idea of unconditional surrender be invoked. Unconditional surrender was introduced in 1944 by Franklin D. Roosevelt. He probably couldn't hear what he was saying at the time. That happens to rulers. But say it he did and it cost a million or so extra lives in the European war. We Allies came to our senses later and permitted Japan to make a conditional surrender, sparing several million more lives. Before Roosevelt, the barbarity of unconditional surrender had almost disappeared from the human ken. Even Genghis Khan, who piled up pyramids of skulls to mark his passage, never so acted until an offer of conditional surrender had been rejected.

In the wars of the new society that I envision, it wouldn't matter much who we fought wars against or even why. These wars would be the pursuit of professional sport by other means, to paraphrase Clausewitz. There would have to be deaths. It wouldn't matter on which side as long as there were dead, but the toll would ideally be kept to about the level of modern killing by automobile on our highways, which reduces the cost to about the level of American involvement in Vietnam. These wars would occur as a response to human nature, specifically male human nature, and would result in many heroic stories being told afterward, some of them true.

These activities—war, storytelling—must, of course, relieve the male of much of the mundane affairs of changing baby nappies and worrying about mortgage payments, but exceptional males would prove they could do both while the rest did muscle jobs and wrote music.

I have run my idea past many women and have yet to find one who gave it the wholehearted embrace that it deserves. This is not because women are stupid (they aren't) or conservative (they are) but because they don't let their minds take in the entire program. Many in fact refuse to listen and walk away.

What I now take the opportunity to tell these women who have deprived themselves of knowledge is that together with doing all the work of society they will also attain all the rewards. They can have all the money, which has never given us men much satisfaction anyway. Life for the dominant female in the society I envision can be one 365-day-a-year shopping spree, and if they choose to imitate Imelda Marcos and buy 2,000 pairs of shoes, a trait for which I admire and respect that Filipina First Lady, so be it.

Women may say that the men would never agree to having their sexual partners buy the yachts and drive the BMWs. They will quote the old saying that the difference between men and boys is the cost of their toys. These are women who have spent insufficient time in heterosexual relationships. To the male, all the material goods he possesses are comparative, the comparison being made with the kids he went to primary school with so many, many years ago. If those peers have thirty-foot cabin cruisers, yes, he will want a thirty-five-footer. However, he will be every bit as happy to paddle a cedar strip canoe while his friends and associates are stuck with lower-price Kevlars. The male ego can be easily satisfied by any female with only a moderate amount of the smarts. A man can almost always be manipulated, and it can happen from a position of female dominance in the same way it happens in conditions of female subservience.

I have not yet thought of a good slogan for my ideal society. "Nothing to lose but your chains" doesn't exactly fit. However, a slogan won't be needed. The idea is far too good, too rational and simultaneously too satisfying to the intuitive side of the brain. We know that like most truly great ideas, it can never come true. We can dream. All the rest is in the lap of the gods and they have so far not done very well.

MESSAGE? WHAT MESSAGE?

AN ELEGANTLY CLEVER ENGLISHMAN named C. Northcote Parkinson wrote a series of sociologic studies in the second half of the twentieth century. His best-known thesis, which became known as Parkinson's law, is that work will always expand to fill the time given for its completion. There followed many more Parkinson laws and one is pertinent to this chapter. Parkinson found that the period when an institution is near collapse and extinction is when it is most famous and erects its finest structures. The British Colonial Office was finally housed in a splendid building in London just when Britain was shedding her entire empire, and the League of Nations buildings in Geneva were completed when the league itself was dead and awaiting burial. The rule of glory too late is perhaps associated with the fact, mentioned elsewhere in this book, that the old apple tree in the orchard produces its biggest crop in its final years, just as Hollywood's noisiest and costliest Academy Awards nights came after there were practically no movies worth awarding. This is the best explanation I can find for calling this the Age of Communication, because communication between one person and another has never been so unreliable.

From a technical point of view, we have never been better off. With a cellular telephone one could, from the upper slopes of Everest, transmit the entire Christian Bible, the budget of the United States or Stephen W. Hawking's study of the Unified Theory in one to two minutes to any place on earth where people willing to read them could be found. But this extraordinary capacity to cram whole mountain ranges of data into peanut shells and send them any place on earth or beyond is merely the mechanics of communication. No matter how good it may be, no matter how much it may and doubtless will be improved, it is not communication and never can be. To suggest otherwise is akin to crediting Gutenberg, the inventor of moveable type for the Europeans, with writing the works of Shakespeare, Molière or Cervantes. There is no evidence he ever wrote anything, not even a grocery list. He provided mechanical means for communicating.

That communication since his time has become a little better and in some ways worse is due to the fact that we have allowed the world's technicians to do a snow job on us. They tell us that since printing, fax and wireless telephone—and now the Internet—are all available and cheap, we communicate better. All this gallimaufry increased with the computer and binary codes. Now these same technicians could demonstrate high-speed communication with computers that would search out and correct grammatical errors, translate into a few score of different languages, take voice commands and answer by voice, and send impeccably correct communication around the world and to the moon, Mars, Saturn and beyond and then back again with a bow tied around it. Why we listened to these nerds and believed them is a sad comment on our gullibility. What we really wanted and needed was to communicate with one another, yet regularly, year in and year out, we saw financial houses crumble, laws perverted and shooting wars begun and lost because vital communication failed at crucial moments. No matter, we just kept telling ourselves that all was well because it was the age of perfect communications.

A copy editor on my old newspaper, the *Vancouver Sun*, expressed the truth. "We are now a multimillion-dollar corporation and we have technical equipment our forefathers couldn't even dream about. But, in the end, this whole massive structure will survive or crash because some copy girl, the lowest paid and least regarded human being in this office, will either carry a piece of paper from one basket to another or will forget to because she had a fight with her boyfriend last night." Many truer words have been spoken, but never before or since on this subject.

Yesterday I needed to research Fibonacci's Golden Mean. Each time you ask the Web search engine called Google for such information, it calculates how much time is used to find it. To find 268 sources of information on the Golden Mean took one tenth of a second. This is the sort of thing that makes us believe we have come a long way in communication since the fur trade days of a couple of hundred years ago. So let us look at the days when Governor George Simpson of the Company of Gentlemen Adventurers Trading Out of Hudson's Bay (we know the company as the Bay) was exploring new trade routes on the rivers of the western mountains. He regularly sent and received mail, done up in oilskin pouches. It was carried across the continent by semi-literate French Canadian and Métis canoemen, over the prairies and across the portages and along the broad Ottawa River that led to Montreal. It took three months to send a message to Montreal and three months for the reply to reach Simpson somewhere in the western mountain tangle. This is not at all like a tenth of a second turnaround. Oh?

Two hundred years ago when the governor's message arrived it was read by the right people. Being in jargon free English, it was understood. The answers were equally prompt and intelligible. Part of the credit for this situation must go to Simpson's character; he was an odd, dumpy little man but contemporaries probably compared him to the offspring of a mating between a parrot and a tiger — not much for looks but when it spoke, everybody listened.

Today, no matter what technology is used, many messages from Vancouver to eastern Canada take more than half a year to obtain a reply and often there is no reply at all because the message was lost, misfiled, misplaced or used to wipe up ketchup from a McDonald's Big Mac that got spilled on a desk. We weren't that much worse off using canoes. By the year 2000, most Canadians weren't getting most messages.

In some other nations communication lasted a bit longer. Many years ago, when we still used typewriters, I tried to order one with a special keyboard from an Ontario agency. Unable to get myself noticed, I picked a totally inadequate address off a label on my machine and wrote to Essen, Germany. I had a reply within ten days. Two months later, I got another reply, in languid prose from their Ontario office. It read as though written by somebody who was a nephew of the general manager. My letter had been drawn to his attention. (Hardly anybody in business today reads letters written to them. If high salaried and somebody's nephew, letters are drawn to their attention, doubtless by a crew of eunuchs who live in those barracks across the railway tracks.) One exception to this dismal scenario was Robert Townsend, who wrote *Up the Organization: How to Stop the Corporation from Stifling People and Strangling Profits*. He turned around the Hertz car rental company largely by doing such things as reading his mail and answering his telephone. But he was exceptional—and is dead.

I cannot resist telling one more story of communication failure in the Age of Communication. This is about an acquaintance in the Northwest Territories who wanted to sell old, abandoned Canol Pipeline steel that ran from the Mackenzie River Valley into the Yukon. He wrote all Canada's steel people but could never gain the courtesy of an acknowledgement to his letters. Like me, he wrote to a broad, general address in Tokyo. They use a different language there and have a funny alphabet but no matter, what did he have to lose? Within two weeks in remote Fort Simpson, a place unknown to practically the entire world until a few years later when the Pope visited, my friend got an offer of a firm contract by mail. The Japanese would take the metal at Tuktoyaktuk on the shores of the Arctic Ocean on specific dates. The dates were specific because, they said, those were the only times when tides were high enough for their ships to enter Tuk harbour. "Not even *I* knew tides in Tuk harbour," said my friend.

I doubt that anybody could get such service today from a German typewriter manufacturer or a Japanese scrap metal company. The correspondence might take only seconds, but to find the person who gave a damn about it might well take more days and months than the matter was worth. Most of the correspondence would go to somebody who knew, with secret joy, that it was not his department and would place it carefully in the circular file beside his right knee.

To this massive communication failure of our age must be added the sad fact, which I dilate upon in another chapter, that the English language is itself so badly damaged that with the best will in the world, communication among the English-speaking people of the world becomes ever more a hit-and-miss proposition.

It is as stupid to blame people for bringing this communication failure about as it is to blame clouds for bringing rain. It happens, that's all. The more complex our world becomes, the less reliable will be communication among us.

We forget all too easily that we do not hear with our ears or see with our eyes. Those are merely devices for carrying electrical impulses to the brain, where seeing and hearing occur. The brain has always screened out most of what we hear and see. If it didn't, we would all be quite mad. A few people, idiot savants we call them, have brains that fail to screen out the unimportant. They can memorize a page of the phone book after a single reading. Usually they end up as recluses, trying to avoid the torrent of facts that pour in upon them; many go insane and most of the rest are less than happy human beings. Our ability to exclude information can be as important as our ability to obtain it.

A simple demonstration of hearing can be conducted at any long, oblong dinner table. You find yourself usually conversing with the person opposite. The conversations of people on your right and left become subdued and are reduced to little more than a mutter. Let diagonal conversations begin, and you will probably screen out the words of the person opposite, who is now also in diagonal dialogue. Good hearing depends far more upon focus than upon loudness or even clarity. None experience this more than people going deaf or people using an unfamiliar language. Once a few words at the beginning of a sentence are lost, the brain's screening mechanism goes into action unbidden and turns all the following words into a mumble. One result is that a deaf person will hear some soft words spoken perfectly well and fail to hear others spoken even more clearly. Those not deaf call it selective hearing, which it is, but the unimpaired don't realize that the screening is an automatic and unbidden response.

The same general rules apply to all the messages we receive. On an average day the resident of a city in North America will be subjected to about 2,000 visual messages. Some will urge him to buy things, others to not violate a red light, others to stop smoking. During the day, he is likely to be conscious of receiving about twenty of these messages, one percent, and at day's end he may remember four or five, either favourably or unfavourably. A special category of message, a scream or a siren, is processed by a different part of the brain and the message is carried by shortcuts to where it is needed. On an ordinary day, most of us don't hear screams or shouts to warn us that we are walking into open manholes, so we process only four or five messages out of the 2,000.

In these circumstances, natural to every human creature, does it really matter how much data my computer can collect in one tenth of a second? Isn't it worth more to realize and live with the fact that in the year 2000 communication among people had become increasingly uncertain and unreliable?

This brings me to a curious situation I encounter each winter, when I live in my Mexican home. People who know that I am fond of that country frequently ask for advice because they, too, are thinking of moving there. I have always offered two pieces of advice. One, do not put money into Mexico you cannot afford to walk away from. Two, try to avoid doing business with Mexicans.

The first answer merely reflects the fact that the international narcotics trade has badly warped Mexican society. Drug cartels now have more money than many of the municipal governments and a few of the state governments. In our state, Sinaloa, the narcotics murder rate is running at the rate of one every twelve hours in a small state of less than two and a half million people, and many of those murdered are policemen, lawyers and judges as well as rival drug lords, pushers and innocent bystanders. This comes close to an open challenge of established government and the outcome of that contest is unclear.

But more pertinent to the subject of this chapter is the stricture to avoid doing business with Mexicans. It seems highly distrustful, at first glance, but it is not. Over decades, I have found the honesty and fair-mindedness of Mexicans to be generally higher than that of Americans and Canadians. By and large, they are unusually honest people. However, their way of doing business is so foreign to the gringo that we sometimes feel they might as well be dishonest.

They have a word for appointment, but few understand it in the terms we do. When a Mexican promises to meet you next Tuesday morning at ten, in the square, what you may not hear is that he is saying that next Tuesday he is likely to be at the square at some time and wouldn't it be nice if your paths crossed? He is startled and dismayed that his gringo friend becomes irritated by noon because he has failed to show up. He feels it should be obvious that there was a birthday party he forgot, an old aunt who got sick or another appointment in a city a hundred kilometres distant that he had forgotten. Mexicans who wait for somebody do not have the equivalent in their language of our English word *wait*. They use the word *hope* instead. "I am hoping for my wife, who is shopping."

Very few Mexicans in rural districts will respond to mail or a telephone message. My house and land is held in trust for me by a major bank. Not once in twenty years have they ever answered a business letter from me. In my Mexican home, I have a telephone with an answering device. There has never been a Mexican who left a message. Many have phoned, many times, they tell me so, but all they get so often is that recorded message. I summon all the patience I possess and am silent. Sometimes it helps to remember occasions up north when an acquaintance and I played telephone tag for a week, leaving messages for one another on answering machines.

Allergic to both paper and electronics, Mexicans end up dealing with you face to face or not at all. Since such meetings are hard to arrange, for reasons listed above, an almost incredible amount of time can be wasted on the simplest of transactions. A neighbour who, like me, had a *fidelcomiso* at a bank, waited five years to get her papers in order, a procedure that in her native state of Wyoming would have occupied a day or two at the most. When she finally obtained them, she complained. The banker said, "Dear Lady, consider how far we have come. In the days of the Spanish king, these papers would have had to go back and forth across the ocean to Madrid and it would have been at least twelve years." She said, "Congratulations. In four centuries you've cut seven years off the time," but he was not amused; she was just another gringo, lacking in common courtesy.

After twenty years, I still have paper problems about my property but, as my banker pointed out, was I ever denied any rights of ownership? (No) Did anyone interfere with my quiet enjoyment of my house and land? (No) And what difference could a few papers make? (Oh, what's the use?)

It is an aversion to this complication of simple processes that prevents me from selling my house on the humid coast and building another in the mountain country where it's springtime twelve months of the year. In my later years, I don't trust myself to keep my temper, and the man who abandons courtesy in Mexico is lost. I shall probably never move.

However, sitting in my patio among the Hibiscus, the Double Hibiscus and the Cup of Gold flowers, I do have the time to consider that the Mexican system is not entirely bad. By keeping communications much as they were in Canada in Governor Simpson's time, the Mexicans have avoided the sensory overload that has made so much of our communication system meaningless.

It is hard to love, hard to adapt to, but in the end the system works, and that is more than can sometimes be said for our hypersonic message system in Canada.

I say this at the end of a solid hour spent trying to get a telephone number from directory assistance in BC, phoning from Boston, Massachusetts. The system is so clever that it recognizes I am phoning from the Atlantic Coast and the only phone number it will provide is a toll-free number, which is unworkable. They call it a free service for all North America, although the company officials have admitted to me that it only works in parts of North America. I pursued this through many operators and supervisors, all of whom confessed that they had no way of obtaining the number I could have obtained had I been in British Columbia, and finally, despairing, I phoned a friend who picked up her BC phone book and read out the number. It seems that nobody in the Telus company's information service can get access to that book.

The number I was trying to discover was the telephone company's own office number.

You're fairly accustomed to being kicked around by age 70, so I never uttered a single profane word during that hour. Now I shall in saying this about the Age of Communication, which will probably provide even worse service to my descendants. "Don't EAT that, Elmer, that's HORSESHIT!"

SEX, MARRIAGE, SWEET WOMEN AND ALL THAT SORT OF THING

WHEN I WAS 55, PERHAPS 60, I forget the year but remember it was one of those languid grey winter Vancouver days when the great melancholy of life falls over the cedar swamps, I read of a public opinion poll that had discovered that a majority of women would rather go shopping than have sex. I recognized this as the end of civilization as I had known it. Up to that time, I considered it a joke to say that a nymphomaniac was a woman who would go to bed with her husband right after having her hair done.

Everything, clearly, was changing and had been in the process of violent upheaval for years but it was only on that mournful day that I felt solid earth shift beneath my feet. Other events should have alerted me. My first wife, one of the world's lovelier creatures, divorced me for reasons having largely to do with male ego and then proceeded, with the perversity natural to her sex, to find another husband with exactly the same failings I had.

In sexual politics, small things had become large by the '70s. There was the fact that half the female reporters at the *Vancouver Sun* got a wedgie in their knickers because I used the word *tit* instead of *teat* in a column. It was a distinction as invisible to me as it is to the *Oxford English Dictionary* and it remains so to this day, but the fuss also remains memorable as a symptom of changing society in which facts, which men favour, gave way to feelings, which tend to be the domain of women, a world where things are so because they are so and that is that and stop arguing.

Alterations of sexual patterns matter rather more than fluctuations of the stock market or the cutting of rain forests. For those who, like me, believe that humans present the only case in which two different species of mammal can mate and produce fertile offspring, and have done so for thousands of generations, the changes in the latter half of the twentieth century were not easy to digest. Some of them still give me heartburn but then, by nature, I am a dreamer and inclined to an absurd sentimentality. This is written today in Sinaloa, Mexico, with a copy of Mazatlan's *Noroeste* newspaper at hand. Mexican newspapers report pretty much what papers all over the western world are reporting, day by day, but Mexican social pages are very, very different from those of the cold northern lands. I never fail to read wedding stories in *Noroeste*. Today, I learn that Fernando and Consuela have agreed to "join their destinies." Elsewhere it is reported of another couple that they have been "Invaded by Love." Yet another señorita "listened to the commands of her heart" when accepting the proposal of her suitor.

Next to finding Oberon, King of the Fairies, dancing at the foot of the garden, translating Mexican newspaper wedding stories from the Spanish comes a close second. "The most beautiful sentiment of which all humanity is capable of feeling, love, united in matrimony Lluvia Selena Hernandez Vargas and Mario Javier Blanco Vergara. This love, sky high, caused them this day to give their oaths to honour and to understand one another for the rest of their lives as a pair."

Another: "Many changes in a human life come about but there is none greater than to be loved. Alma Rosa Diaz Fajardo experienced this change and departed from her solitary life to change into a wife, companion and friend, in short, to begin a new path as the bride of Mario Betancourt."

Will he forever remember to lift the toilet seat? Don't ask.

"Our Lord Jesus Christ was the special guest at the ceremony in which Elizabeth Madrado Freeman and Rigoberto Castaneda Allcantrara decided to unite their lives in the indissoluble bonds of matrimony."

Indissoluble? It might be noted that in Mexico the divorce rate is climbing, year by year, toward our level in this country of almost 40 percent, but we deal here not with crude facts but with that thing called love. Mexican editors use the word *love* with what can only be described as wild abandon. Their counterparts in the US and Canada, conscious that taste is all a matter of public acceptance, use the word charily, after much consideration and discussion among the staff. They are more at ease putting the word *fuck* on their pages.

Further as to style, the Mexican social pages have never heard of orgasm and make only indirect reference to the act of penetration, the latter long after the wedding by a report revealing that this lady or that is expecting "a visit from the stork." Although I have not yet had the pleasure of spotting it, I have no doubt that some Mexican editor has used the old Victorian euphemism, announcing that this or that wife is about to provide her husband with "proof of her affection." Alas, no Mexican paper has yet reported a marriage being consummated in the vestry, as is supposed to have happened once in an English newspaper. There remains no doubt that Mexican editors are in tune with their readers in using prose so heavy in flowers, hearts and absurd dreams and I, for one, am with the Mexican editors. What's life without illusions?

I have said this at considerable length, and gone off to another country to find my material, so the reader may know where I come from. Like most men, I am as sentimental as most women are practical and I find this trait hard to shed.

That some of my sentimentality has been lost matters less than that many of the rock-solid beliefs I held have melted away. No doubt many of them should have—perhaps all. Remember, I was raised to believe that men were breadwinners and wives were support staffs and children were what happened and continued to happen even after you found out what was causing them, even after you reached the point of seeing that old King Herod was not entirely wrong. For many years I took the position that it was time enough for women to demand equality when they learned to squeeze a toothpaste tube from the bottom. In my first political campaign, when Liberal party strategists warned the candidates that Women's Lib should not be treated lightly, I looked forward to responding to a question about whether I favoured women joining the liberation movement by answering, "Of course, provided she has her husband's permission." Nobody asked and I never was able to drop that clanger, the one thing that might have made me worth noticing in the metropolitan press and lost me the election.

That and many old ideas now seem strange. However, at any point in history, the views of a generation or two ago seem strange and sometimes verge on incomprehensibility. Ask any traditional American of the Old South whose daughter has married a black man.

Human nature is very slow to change for there are impulses in everybody's genes that were built up over millennia, as is detailed later in this chapter. Human behaviour, however, has been changing with remarkable frequency ever since we stopped dragging our knuckles on the ground as we walked. Humans do change, often for the better. The reason is usually, although not always, external, and I am not referring to the Great Reformer in the Sky as the force responsible for all this change but to such things as weather, gamma rays and other causes discovered by scientists.

When I first encountered the idea that females had a natural right to fly fighter bombers and join commando garrotting classes, I did the first thing that came to mind, I grew a beard, one of the few things women cannot accomplish. Later I thought on the matter a bit more deeply.

I am still sentimental and probably will be forever. I still don't think women should be in combat roles in the armed services. They are designed to create and nurture life, not to destroy it. And I do salute that thing called love. But love is not the subject of this chapter. Sex is. We have too frequently treated sex as if it were the same thing as love.

I have not lost interest in the subject of sex and never will, and no one will hear me utter that silly old dictum that sex is a vastly overrated pastime. It is seldom rated highly enough. It is the main source of life's glorious confusions and without it we'd be a poor, drab lot.

We try to equate it with love and a common name for sexual union is "making love." Maybe, but not necessarily. Sex is allied to love, it mingles with love and it sometimes leads to a semipermanent form of love, but it is separate from love. There's physical proof of this in every coitus. No matter what tender attention preceded it, at the moment of orgasm, the partners retreat into themselves to experience the pleasure all alone.

As for importance, love is, of course, immensely more important than sex. Love is the most important thing in the universe in all its many forms—between parents and children, young lovers, old lovers and friends. It is so important I may never attempt to deal with it in this book, any more than I am likely to try to deal with the question of whether the universe is eternal. Love is a force like no other. For the moment, I confine myself to the discussion of sex, personality and the mould that a million years of evolution cast for us.

Nature, God or whatever power there be that has a good sense of humour decided that our species could best survive and prosper if there was a continuous mixing of the gene pool. As a poet whose name I forget said, "Then nature pulled the greatest wheeze / by turning out both hes and shes." What, other than sex, produces so much laughter, which, God knows, we need.

The power of sex is probably not as universal as old Dr. Fraud of Vienna, fugleman for the chattering classes, pretended to discover with the research now revealed to be largely bogus. But the sex drive is tremendously strong and, like organized religion, when obstructed or perverted it can produce calamitous evils.

To the greatest extent possible, we shouldn't obstruct the impulse that, in the second half of the twentieth century, science succeeded in making readily available to us with practically no penalty payments. Now, more than ever, we should not try to surround sex with religion or other mysticisms. Now we should know that it is more fun than jogging and easier to learn than golf. If any of my descendants reading this have remained virgins in their mature years, I urge them to remedy the situation quickly. Let the younger ones know what parents mean when they say their young are not yet able to handle sex emotionally. That is grown-up talk for saying that you are likely to take it too seriously. There is such a time in everyone's life, but older people tend to try to prolong it unreasonably.

As for the calamitous evils, most of us are inoculated against them. Incest is not good, it defeats the program of mixing different genes to produce different babies. But it is a small concern because humans are programmed to reject sexual encounters with siblings. A natural prohibition, always better than a man-made one, it keeps almost all of us from all forms of incest.

It's our bad luck that this aversion to intercourse with people too familiar to us extends into the longer marriages that medicine made possible for us last century. For most of human history, marriages were short because widows and widowers were created so soon. Now husbands and wives who may be perfectly compatible have far too many years of togetherness, and familiarity induces the incest prohibition. Nobody's perfect, not even such planners as God. Either that or this happenstance is a signal that we are all living too long and perhaps should be arranging a system whereby farewell parties are arranged for everybody's seventieth birthday. Make it eightieth.

We would enjoy sex and endure marriage much better if we began with a few truths. One is that men and women are neither equal nor the same. Ask any old couple who are celebrating their sixtieth wedding anniversary if they ever believed that men and women were the same. (Ask soon; before long there won't be any to ask.) The sexes are different as boys and girls and different throughout almost all the adult years. Only in extreme old age do they tend to become a bit more similar, with aggressive men becoming gentler and gentle women becoming more aggressive. They still don't reach equality any more than do apples and oranges or dogs and cats. Alan Holbrook said it well: "Women and cats do as they damned well please, and men and dogs had best learn to live with it."

One of our mistakes of the past century was co-education, putting boys and girls together for no reason other than they were going to be together in adult life. Both sexes were harmed and still are. Soon after infancy passes, girls are more mature socially than boys and ready for teachings that boys are not. Boys have their own virtues, and no reasoning known to God or man should oblige them to fit a semi-female pattern.

So they are going to be together in adulthood? Yes, you got that right. They will. Nature will take care of it, without any intervention by the rulers. The state won't even have to pass laws or issue instruction sheets. What separate education can accomplish is to make each sex learn more about what interests them in other fields of human endeavour, and faster.

Kingsley Browne says it clearly in his book *Divided Labours*. Gender inequality is inevitable, he says, because of our evolutionary heritage. Females invest resources in rearing their children and men aggressively compete with one another for access to the females. Such hormonal patterns were hard-wired into our brains during those millions of years after we came down from the trees and went out on the grasslands. A few thousand years of civilization is but an eyelid's blink, far too short a time for changing basic patterns.

Among the patterns: Women, weaker physically although in no other way, had to use their wits to avoid being trampled. Their voices are higher, like children's voices, because the males of any species are reluctant to harm the young. Men, as hunters—and we have almost always been hunters; eating farmed vegetables began only yesterday, in the afternoon—needed a good spatial sense. Women, as manipulators of the physically stronger individuals, became better talkers. Women have a better sense of smell (safe food for the children) and men are better at matters technical such as making tools or building shelters.

Men are expendable. One woman can produce only a limited number of children but one man can father several hundred children. It follows that men take more risks and, in a country such as Mexico, the men are fifteen times more likely to die in accidents than women are.

Males are, for all practical purposes apart from hitting other people, weaker. The male is, in fact, an aberration of the female sex. We all began in the womb as females but the X chromosome turned a little more than half of us into males, although, because of male weaknesses, the proportion in the general population is soon reversed in favour of females. In times of war, obeying commands still hidden from science, women produce an excessive number of male babies and the war has to take care of reducing the number to below 50 percent.

In coming eons the male, being short a chromosome or two, will probably go down the one-way street to nowhere, like the blue-eyed people, produced with another recessive gene. The females will still be there, brown-eyed all of them, perhaps, but still there.

A factor in male-female human relationships is that the females bear offspring that are only partially formed. Babies have bulbous heads with a hole on top of the skull and disproportionately small arms and legs. Many parts of them are not fully developed for years. The eyes, among the last, don't complete full development until twenty or more years after birth. Humans are little more than embryos when first let out into the air and cannot care for themselves within an hour, a week, a month or a year. In the case of devoted professional university students, thirty-five years and more. In the infant stage humans have a sweet, milky smell. I never liked them. A father must remind himself that in time they'll grow up to be as good as he is, and his hidden instincts help by convincing him that these ugly little creatures are what living is all about because everybody says so.

Because women required help during the years of child-bearing, the male had to take on the task of supporting her. To this day he's not sure exactly why but, aided by instinct, he has accepted the notion for hundreds of thousands of years.

When we became civilized we institutionalized this human characteristic and the male became responsible for the female he impregnated by the force of law and religion. Religion had little to do with the matter for the first many centuries of Christianity but a Roman Catholic bishop introduced the idea of lifetime marriage as a religious duty. He took an entirely practical, if little known view of the matter. He perceived that men were using up too much of their imaginative time in seeking new females to impregnate. Better, he reasoned, that a male be required to cohabit with one woman indefinitely. Any man who had to live with the same woman for long would inevitably become so bored that he would look elsewhere for fulfillment and might be expected to find it in religious studies.

The impulse of the female is to find a strong male as a protector of herself and her family. He should not be the most aggressive male. Females tend to admire the macho male but are reluctant to choose one as a permanent mate. Behind this rational analysis there lurk other impulses that emerge at the strangest times. However, let us confine ourselves to the obvious for the moment.

The impulse of the male is to impregnate as many females as possible and if a show of strength or security is the way to obtain this, he will so display, honestly or dishonestly. Posturing, boasting and vainglory are as natural to him as an erection, to which they are related.

The female, seeking to give birth to the strongest and best, is aware that she is fallible. Above all else, she is practical and recognizes that no man is what he pretends to be when wooing her. She may have been fooled and she is practical enough to sense it. At this point, usually unconsciously, she thinks of trying another male's sperm and at these times she is apt to choose a partner who is lousier, more brutal, more foolishly macho than her mate. Few people think this through, but it is common enough for women from good and happy marriages to run off with louts. To quote Finley Peter Dunne's famous Martin Dooley, "Many a successful mandolin artist has seen his wife run off with a professional boxer." The impulse to take a wild lover peaks when the female is most fertile, an explanation of the surprisingly large number of English fathers who, DNA testing showed, had not sired all the children they thought to be theirs.

The male view is, of course, the simpler one—just bed as many of them as you can and dare. Most of us are unaware of this old evolutionary programming in our heads, but some nationalities are much more practical about the matter than ours. Mexicans are much more honest, although not more open. Day to day they're a prudish lot. The following story will serve.

At a dinner party, bilingual, I made the remark that something I had engaged in, probably a duck shoot, was the most fun I had ever had with my clothes on. A widow lady, Dona Mercedes, said her English wasn't quite good enough to catch the significance of that remark.

"Dona Meche," I said, "you were married. You had children. You have to know what it is to have fun with your clothes off."

She answered frostily. "My husband and I were very much in love. That didn't mean I had to take off my clothes in front of him." I was tempted to say, "Close your eyes and think of the Republic," but didn't.

They may be a prudish lot, but the Mexicans are in many ways more open and honest than the gringos. Wives recognize that fooling around with girls is a secondary male characteristic, like hair on the face. Many Mexican men have second families by women called "second fronts," and sometimes the first and second families meet only at the father's funeral.

What is usually maintained in Mexico is the family unit, both the official and unofficial one. Mexicans were polled a few years ago as to who they trusted. Surprising and gratifying to some, the army scored more than 50 percent, much higher than the police. Lawyers, newspapermen and other such types were, as usual elsewhere, near the bottom. But 87 percent of all the Mexicans (yes, yes, yes, don't be tiresome, nineteen times out of twenty) said they could trust their families. Almost any observer will attest that it is the wives who weld the family unit together.

English wives are almost as wise as Mexican wives. They rejected the impossible American dream of marriage. Somerset Maugham, a writer so good he never won a prize, said, "American women expect to find in their husbands a perfection that English women only hope to find in their butlers."

In Canada and the United States the impossible dream of stable marriage, working husband, happy wife and obedient children, most of whom chafed under the rules, remained officially alive and even apparently healthy for a decade or more after the Second World War. The pill changed it all.

Men used to say that the trouble with women was that we had invented too many labour-saving devices for the home — dishwashers, washer/dryer combos and robot vacuum cleaners. We had given women too much time to think. This wasn't what freed them. Yes, they had time to think, but for a long time they didn't have a means of escape from the bonds of caring. If they had children, they needed male support when the children were young. If they were single they had to avoid having children and, alas, the less able they were to provide for such little strangers the more likely they were to have them. Suffragettes were not free women. A change far more important than getting the vote was required and it, too, became common all over the world. Abortion.

There have always been induced abortions, just as there have always been mercy killings, but for many centuries both were done quietly and illegally, which is possibly better than publicly with noise. The need for legal abortion will always be there as long as there are rapes, incest cases and women who have that lamentable inability to associate cause with effect and who use abortion as the ultimate birth control device.

Most western nations have now made it legal to get rid of the unwanted, provided the unwanted are helpless to defend themselves. Abortions save many women from miserable, unhappy lives and, although anti-abortionists will deny it, they also save many children from lives so bereft of all goodness and love that they may be far better off among the unborn dead. But some unpalatable truths about the morality of it all remain, which most of us have not yet faced. We kill unwanted babies, who have clearly done harm to no one, while sparing psychopathic killers who have done terrible harm to many people. Is it logical? Of course not, but many things aren't.

When I was a Member of Parliament in '68 to '73, I used to receive ill-tempered letters from people who wanted unlimited abortion on demand. I would always reply by welcoming their letter because the question was so troubling, being associated, as it was, with the question of capital punishment for criminals. Would my correspondent please let me know her stand on hangings? No such letter was ever answered, which is one of the reasons that mass write-in letters to MPs are a waste of everybody's time. Paying attention to write-in programs is like seeking rational discussion with an oyster, in case they be granted the vote one of these days. MPs also learn early that the radicals of any movement—feminist, abortionist, anti-abortionist, ecologist and flat earth society—soon become raging pains in the ass and are so recognized by their own supporters, who desert the organizations they joined when saner folk were in command. Left alone, radicals will almost always wither and drop off the branch before ripening.

Here we are at the millennium's turn with most families in Canada settling for 1.6 infants. That's not enough to avert population decline. Neither Canadians nor Americans now reproduce themselves, and both countries depend upon immigration for population growth. Some nations, such as post-Franco Spain, are losing 30 percent of their population with each generation. Statisticians have calculated that the Swedes are going to eventually disappear from the planet.

Thus the new age.

The year 2002 woman has now little need for a male to nourish and protect her during her procreative years. A woman with a share of the smarts can hire males for that brief time when nature makes her vulnerable. Where is a more prominent example than our former prime minister, the late Pierre Trudeau, who was always trendy? At the lady's request, he fathered a child by a woman who is a practising lawyer and didn't want marriage. She did, however, want his child and it carries his name and, in the later years of his life, his deep affection and attention.

Add to this, of course, the many women who have decided they will have no children, at any time, with anybody. In pursuit of that subject, I wrote the following newspaper column, directed to a young yuppie woman who wears flat-heeled shoes.

> Dear Eve,
>
> This is in response to your fresh, open, sprightly and intelligent recent letter in which you announced that you and your Significant Other have chosen to live childless.
>
> I am reminded of Mark Twain, who, in response to the question "What...would the people of the world be without women?" answered "Scarce...mighty scarce."
>
> You put forward many reasons for never becoming a mother. Most of them are excellent,

none more so than your statement that babies repel you and you lack motherly instincts. This is true of some women. Precious few, but there are some.

If your distaste for small humans is real, it's best that you have none. Kids don't lack many material things in our world, but a shocking number lack good old-fashioned love in their home, and when love isn't there, hateful emotions often take its place.

You offer other rational arguments against motherhood.

Canada, you say, doesn't need more people. We might be happier with fewer. You also say, understandably, that you do not believe you have any patriotic duty to raise sons to fight wars for us.

Babies, you say, are bound to interfere with your career. For a good part of your productive years you would face a dilemma: the prospect of becoming an occasional part-time professional or, if you should choose to devote as much attention to your work after children arrive as now, doing so with guilt because you would know the children would suffer for it. As you wisely say, so-called quality time are chattering class words, used usually by people who are damaging their children by divorce but don't want to face the truth.

Quality time is humbug. It proposes that concentrated contact with children, at times of the adult's choice, can substitute for the constant reassuring presence of an adult in the home. Children do not have neat schedules printed in their busy little heads. The notion they will save their cuts, bruises, fears, horrors and heartaches for a scheduled quality time is an adult fantasy, born of guilt.

So you are being clear-eyed and honest. Your country doesn't need more children, you don't want them and you can, you say, do more good in the world by using a portion of your handsome income to help the many underprivileged children already born. The money you would spend carrying a pair of kids from birth through college would be a gift of the gods to about fifty children in parts of Africa.

Well, I could add to your list of reasons. I've been the father to four children, three of whom already have families of their own. It wasn't roses all the way. Measles, sibling rivalries, quarrelling, the ever present threat of drug abuse, alcohol or wild driving and bad company, not to even mention the threat of forty or fifty character-warping catastrophes for which, the psychiatrists would tell us, we were to blame—that's fun? Often you want to drop out of parenting, by being temporarily embalmed if necessary, returning twenty years later when your children are all adults.

Oddly enough, when they do leave home a new and unexpected unease intrudes. It would be ludicrous to call their departures ingratitude. They have gone out to make their own lives. That's how it should be. However, the transition is not easy for the father and mother. Children stop being children, but parents never stop being parents.

So what I should say is that you have made a very wise decision. I should, but I cannot. Your decision may be good but remember that neither you nor I nor anyone else can alter the reproductive urge born into us all. Plants, porpoises or university professors, a hidden voice tells us that we are not and can never be a single individual whose life begins at birth and ends at death. Although we do not clearly understand it, we sense that in our species our lifetime is just a bridge arching between dead yesterdays and unborn tomorrows. Every living creature feels this.

The old tree in the orchard fruits most prolifically just before it dies, impelled by that innate demand that it reproduce itself.

This isn't always or necessarily a good thing. How is our world better because of the survival instincts of the Norway rat, the house fly or the malaria *Plasmodium* parasite? Leave that question to the priests. I say only one thing: the urge is there, as much a part of us as our bones and blood.

Choosing to be childless, dear Eve, is not a decision like choosing your hair colour or even choosing a career. You swim against a primal tide.

Remember also that you were born with all the eggs you will ever have. Each month you lose one and someday they will all be gone, but an instinct within you may not.

We have entered a society where females choose male partners for fun as often as forever and many females change partners often, again for fun. In such a society the male role is being reduced to just squirting a bit of sperm here and there, and it is a depressing thought for us that this is the role of a bull on a cattle ranch. Bovine bulls are invariably insensitive, awkward, fat and stupid.

It can be only a few years before family naming will change in our world. Since the Middle Ages, the English-speaking world has required a woman to take the name of her husband and family lineage has been traced through the male line. Recently laws have changed. In British Columbia wives retain their father's name, which they mistakenly call a maiden name. They now must take action to change it to their husband's surname and fewer each year bother. The time for more change is near and perhaps here.

In future we may expect all children to take the mother's surname, the name of each father of her children being an add-on. The daughter of Mary Smith will thus go through life as Samantha Smith-Jones and Samantha's daughter's son will be Robert Smith-McIvor or McWhatever.

Royalty may retain the patrilineal system a bit longer. Royalty is always slower to change. For most people the time for matrilineal naming was yesterday or, at the latest, today.

Several West Coast aboriginal societies were matrilineal. Provided there is general agreement, it is as good a system as any for the purpose of inheritance and for avoidance of marriages of near relatives.

Thus it can be seen that the male is no longer head of the western family, and if you think I resent that change you get full marks because I do. I liked being head of a family. I liked a society that honoured me if I did well in that role. I liked solid families that lasted a long time. So do police officers, who can testify to the crime that arises in the broken family and in the one-parent home. This is not a book about what I like, it is about the realities—the realities of societal change and also the realities of evolutionary sexual instincts, which may be different.

Research has been uncovering some extraordinary truths about our programming. A small example is a study that showed that women choose sexual partners by, among other things, smell. To condense a lengthy study into a few sentences: All human bodies reject the invasion of foreign substances, which is why Sir William Osler said, "Given a chance, the body will always heal itself." If this is true, why don't women's bodies reject fetuses, half of whose genes are foreign? Often the female body does exactly that: it is called natural abortion. Usually the female body does not because it has a protective device that tells the body not to expel those particular foreign elements in the womb. The safety of the fetus is best preserved by a particular mismatching of the female's genes with the male's. The male genes should not be too much like her father's. Research at the University of Bern, Switzerland, in 1995 showed that college women who sniffed sweaty T-shirts of men they never saw almost invariably chose the scent of men whose genes were most likely to provide a successful pregnancy. The only women who could detect no difference were those taking the pill, a situation so striking that it might convince some people that there must be a God who runs everything.

Nature, not nurture, is what preserves the permanent differences between the sexes. They are natural and like other things natural, we should adapt to them, not try, vainly, to alter them by intellectual exercises.

The female tends to be right brained. She absorbs information from a hundred or a thousand sources, usually unintentionally, and leaps to conclusions, which are sometimes wrong. The male, left brained, figures. Except in daydreaming, he is less likely to leap to a wrong conclusion. His impulse is to deal with provable verities. The square of the hypotenuse is always going to equal the sum of the squares of the other two sides and he likes it that way.

Beginning with the Industrial Revolution, our societies have tended to favour left-brained people and left-brained thinking, to the disadvantage of women and also North American Natives, who, like women, tend to think intuitively. Scientists say this is now altering, in part because of television, which, unlike reading, is a right-brained activity.

There is, of course, a contradiction in the above.

Having said in another chapter that women should be running the world because they are so sensitive and also practical, how can this be reconciled to the fact that they act so often on intuition, which cannot always be correct? Having said that males are better at spatial relationships and other linear thinking, how can I suggest that they should be writing poetry and telling imaginative stories to the grandchildren?

You asked the question. I'll tell you the answer. I don't know.

I know this. I like women. I like their soft, perfumed bodies. I like their high voices. I like the way they wave their hands when they talk and I like their quick comprehension of complicated human affairs.

I like their laughter. I like their impulsive fun. I even like them when they go shopping. I like seeing Madame de Pompadour and Mother Eve sometimes peep out from under their curly eyelashes. There are times I even enjoy their deviousness. It's a quality they developed to protect themselves against the stronger and sometimes violent males but they all use it, from time to time, not because they need to but just for practice, keeping their hand in in case they need it some other time.

So many women come to the imagination.

An old woman, her face lined like the sand dunes of the Sahara, rolling dough gently and murmuring, "I also make love this way." A kid, yes, a kid, who possesses The Look. When she encounters a male of any age her look says, "You and me, there is something special between you and me. We know something that nobody else on earth understands." She will grow up to marry the chief executive of IBM or become the world's most expensive prostitute or, perhaps, encounter a tragedy she cannot understand. Meanwhile she will have brightened the day of every male who comes near her. Women, who are often less than kind to each other, are apt to say she knows exactly what she is doing. I doubt it but maybe. I don't care. I smell roses.

I think, too, of the old mother of Stephen Hawking, the brilliant physicist who has brought us close to the Unified Theory of the Universe. Interviewed on TV, she said, "Of course some of Stephen's ideas are absurd, but we all have some crazy ideas."

Sex is more available to everybody now. In a sense, the generations since 1960 have put the act in its proper place. I grew up in an age when it was treated by the young with sniggers. Boys asked which girls did and which girls didn't. You married one kind and enjoyed the other. It was a lot of twaddle, encouraged by parents, most of whom had never learned anything other than the missionary position. One of my great regrets are the girls I did not bed, although looking back, I recognize now that that was exactly what they had in mind. Oh well.

So far I have talked of nothing except the differences between the sexes and their habits on the mattress. I have sought to distance sex from love, although they cannot be completely separated. Sex is wild, funny, tricky and accounts for much of the natural insanity of our days and years. However, I cannot close without addressing the subject of love once more.

I have known these lovers for fifteen years.

Maria was standing behind a door when good looks were being passed out. She is short, squat and fat. Her lower jaw sticks out. Her complexion is muddy. In the game of good looks, she was never dealt any card higher than a trey. She is uneducated and lives in a Mexican village in a little house of concrete bricks. Her husband is Juan. He is a fisherman and also has little education or skills beyond those of a fisherman. He is unusually good-looking—his features are bold, his hair has a wave and his voice has a good lift to it.

Twenty-five years ago, Juan kidnapped Maria. They were both in their teens but she, like Shakespeare's Juliet, was not yet

14 and her family talked darkly about getting the police. In the end they didn't.

Juan and Maria have lived on the hard crisp edge of poverty for most of the years since. The longer they are together, the more closely they are identified with each other. In the village they never speak of one of them; it is always Maria and Juan, as we say bacon and eggs, fish and chips, Adam and Eve.

Their unending passion was for a child, but she could never have one. She frequently became pregnant and friends held their breath to see if she could carry the fetus but always she lost the child, usually in the first trimester. Once, when everybody tiptoed around her, she kept it for seven months but then it was born dead.

All Juan said was, "My wife is fat and ugly and she can't make babies for me, but when my wife laughs my entire world glows." *Todo mi mundo es incandense.*

The secret of their love may be the laughter. I don't know. I don't claim to understand love, I just know it to see it. Maria, whom most people would think has had little to laugh about, laughs a great deal. She laughs at herself, at Juan and at the whole world. She is witty. She tells great jokes. Juan, a quieter person, sits back while she talks, smiling, feeling the glow from her. Juan has had no mistresses.

It is not exactly *Romeo and Juliet* but it is exactly love, and unlike Shakespeare's this story has a happy ending. Twenty years after Juan kidnapped her, Maria finally had a baby boy, Francisco, a bright, healthy kid now in school. Perhaps he wonders sometimes why his home is so much happier than other homes in the village.

When skies go grey and the dreary chill of November creeps into the marrow of the bone I think of that family and then I know that in this foolish and often nasty world there remains always love, to make glad the heart of man.

There Is Life After Television

Yes, there is life after television just as there is sex after marriage, information that will delight some people and astonish others.

Movies and television did immense harm to western nations during the twentieth century, albeit more subtly than the scourges of unconditional surrender wars, AIDS and terrorism. Atomic bombs, wars and the rest were dreadful, but none of them warped man's spirit or weakened his soul as did the flickering screen.

There were, as with any art forms, exceptions, but by century's end the movie industry was reduced to dependence upon shock, horror and general depravity to grab public attention. Although mankind has emerged as effective rulers of this planet, in many ways we remain the timid, weak little creature we were for millions of years. The emotion most easily aroused is fear, closely allied with anger and the urge to violence; the last to be aroused are love, humour and the instinct to charity. Hollywood built a huge industry on this knowledge of the mind's workings. Anger and violence are easier to write, act, direct and produce. They are profitable. They sell. One of the few growth industries during the Great Depression of the 1930s and continuing for the rest of the century, movies served as the people's opium.

Television, which arrived in the 1950s, was similarly pernicious, but its worst effects were mitigated by a natural triviality in almost all that it presented. The great evil it visited on the world was that it made all things cheap and meretricious. Three generations of our people were taught that the artificial is better than what is real, TV's producers, unlike God, having public opinion polls to tell them what to create. They created what a majority of the people could never bestir themselves to oppose or criticize.

The bland led the bland. A story that may be apocryphal but is believable is about radio, sometimes called television with the picture off. In designing the launch of a new station in a major city, the developers polled the citizens to learn all the things they did not like about the radio stations then serving the community. The new station avoided every one of these features in its programs. At the end of a year, this had worked, in a sense, in that the new station was never criticized. However, the opinion polls showed that nobody could remember ever tuning it in. In becoming inoffensive it had made itself invisible, which is not what people in the business of selling advertising prefer.

Thanks to television, we were taught to think in fifteen-second sound bites, later reduced to ten—an exciting picture and somebody uttering a couple of catch phrases. Anything too complex to be shown or explained in less than thirty seconds was unacceptable and after a time a great many people thought that such problems could not exist. The effect on democratic processes has been frightful, for the politicians have been encouraged to tailor their every action and decision to what will sell on the evening news broadcast, and both politicians and people have been deluded into thinking that there are no solutions to human ills other than simple, short solutions, a manifest absurdity.

The ascendancy of the artificial over the real may be observed by anybody attending a public ceremony in which they have a choice of watching human beings talking to them or watching the same people speaking to them simultaneously from a television screen. Wherever the television sets are provided, most people will turn to them rather than to real life.

Of course, public good accompanied both film and television. Television monitors made homes and factories safer. Both TV and film were valuable teaching aids. Instead of half a dozen students clustering around for a poor view of their instructor assembling some delicate part, 100,000 students could watch on a screen and see it displayed much more clearly, for their purposes, than in real life. For all the abundance of bad stories badly told, film and TV occasionally carried good stories badly told and even the ultimate, seldom attained on stage, on film or in print, good stories well told. There may even have been advances in the portrayal of news events, although it is a bit hard to see how any important human cause was advanced by watching Lee Harvey Oswald assassinated or a passenger plane flying into one of the World Trade Center towers. These and other minor advances were never enough to offset the general harm done to the social fabric.

Only toward the end of the twentieth century did we see some awakening from this dream world. Television sets continued to blaze and blare in several rooms of the average home, but it was observable that much of the time nobody watched and among most of the watchers, nobody cared. It had become a background sound and light display.

Then came the 500 channel television universe and the major networks became just another set of players in the game, distinguished from the rest only by having more money to play with.

At this critical moment came the Internet, in which people do not become observers, critical or, more often, uncritical of what they see; they are now the participants. There have been few more hopeful developments in my lifetime. Our situation resembles to a remarkable degree the situation when the nineteenth century was becoming the twentieth, the Victorian age of charades in the front parlour, homemade music and barbershop quartets in the park. Men were more interested in playing sports than watching them. Mankind must have entertainment, it is fundamental to our nature, but far too soon in the twentieth century we began to buy the stuff mass produced rather than making our own. Mass production is good for cars and watches but not for song, dance and story.

Therefore the arrival of the participatory Internet is an event of profound importance, the full effects of which I would be foolish to try to predict. So I won't.

I have high hopes, however, that the twentieth century's two most vitiating inventions have wreaked their worst upon us and that, having foolishly given away our power to create art, we are now on the verge of taking that power back.

THE VILE BRUTE WITHIN

AMBROSE BIERCE—AMBROSE THE GREAT, as I think of him—wrote, "In every man's heart there is a lion, a pig, an ass and a nightingale. Differences in their distribution account for variations of character." The time has come to speak about the pig or, more accurately, the baboon, our cousin among the apes. Although man is not descended from apes and monkeys and no evolutionist ever claimed he is, they are our near relatives in the animal world and they have many of our characteristics, including curiosity, humour, playfulness and the urge to experiment. None, however, are as close to human in behaviour as the baboons, which are noted for being mean, shifty, selfish, greedy and cruel. Baboons are a nasty race and so are we, beneath a thin gloss we paint over ourselves and call civilization.

Baboons are almost the opposite of wolves, who have so many characteristics we are taught to admire, such as love of family, independence of spirit and natural dignity. It has always caught my fancy that the wolves, which kill other animals with savagery and an utter indifference to their suffering (they regularly feed on a downed steer while it is still alive), never attack human beings. The wolf seems to have a prohibition in his gene pattern that prevents him from harming men, which no doubt contributed to the more numerous sub-race of wolves, the domestic dog.

The dog actually seems to love us but the wolf goes only so far as to resist ever doing us harm. The shared characteristic of these two canine groups has always seemed to me to be about the highest recommendation of humans there is.

We are told that all this is anthropomorphism and, as a long word usually indicates, something detrimental to us. We should not talk of cruelty, greed or any other human characteristic in animals, who are merely being animals and have no understanding of morals. The trouble with that argument is that it isn't true. We, too, are animals, and although we have developed strong habits of behaviour in the areas of decency, honour, faithfulness and the rest, we can shake them all off in a matter of moments, and all too often we do.

If this collection is to have any merit for the people who read it fifty or a hundred years from today, or five, six or seven, it must acknowledge one terrible truth: there is a mean and nasty streak in man. All men. We are, at times, a vile lot, and the evil is not learned, it is ingrained in us.

Christians are not my favourite people, still less my favourite philosophers, but for all their fanciful religious tales and taboos, they often come closer to the fundamentals than other cults. In this, they did so with the concept called original sin. Man, they said, is born with evil in him. We may submerge it, divert it, overcome it or, by thinking about baseball games and duck shooting instead, sublimate it. It remains, it is part of our character, a foulness that, like the smell of a septic tank, can be covered over but never eradicated.

The trouble with liberals is that they think this basic human flaw can be removed by reform legislation. The trouble with conservatives is that they think original sin is here to stay and we shouldn't meddle with anything so old and well established. The trouble with socialists is... oh well, it's 2002 and everybody knows that socialism is wrong although nobody can say exactly why, except that all socialist governments get defeated. If you would rather be right than president, keep out of socialist parties. Keep out of them all, for that matter, and find a different trade.

It is a simple, provable fact that man has some terrible impulses in his very bloodstream. Men have not only a hatred of other men, they go further than mere murder and take pleasure in torturing and humiliating their victims.

Genocide occurred many times during the twentieth century. The Armenians in Turkey, the Jews in Germany and more recently the Tutsis in Africa all testify to that. But what happened was nothing new. The Christian Bible speaks with apparent approval of genocides conducted by the tribes of Israel (see, for example, Esther 8:11). Genocide is war carried to extremes.

I was, in a small way, involved in a genocide project when I joined the Royal Canadian Air Force in 1941, intending to become a bomber pilot. Whatever the revisionists may prefer to believe today, we knew our task was to flatten the cities of Germany so the government would surrender. There wasn't one of us who believed that those cities had been emptied of women, children and other non-combatants. This was to be our method of forcing Germany to surrender—killing civilians and making their cities uninhabitable. People who say they have no such recollection of the Second World War are either very stupid or are lying.

Genocide is regrettable, but it is the viler aspects of human nature, often released by it, that we do not care to examine.

There has been such an examination. Find, read and think about the Milgram experiments, conducted at New Haven in 1961, before such information has been shoved down the Memory Hole by Big Brother and removed from the past as well as from present and future. Politically correct people have always complained about the experiment, whose results they did not like.

A cross-section of New Haven people, about 300 ordinary citizens, agreed to take part in a scientific experiment, headed by Stanley Milgram of Yale University. A putative victim, an actor, was placed in an apparently electrified chair. He could be seen and heard by the individuals of New Haven, all of whom had volunteered to take part in the study with no knowledge of what it involved. On instructions from the director of the study, they administered electric shocks to the man in the chair. The shocks varied from very mild, at which the actor merely twitched, to strong, at which he cried out, pleaded that the experiment stop and shouted that he could stand no more, to the ultimate 450-volt shock, marked as DANGER in red on the switching apparatus, which caused the actor to slump into apparent unconsciousness.

Many taking part in the experiment protested when severe or dangerous shocks were ordered. They were urged to continue, lest they spoil the experiment, and always were assured that the experiment's directors took total responsibility for what was happening. Such assurance, with a few repetitions, was enough for two-thirds of the people to complete the entire series of shocks up to the point where it appeared they might be killing the subject. They resisted all pleas for mercy from the man in the chair. A few giggled while applying pain, one or two others appeared to take pleasure in what they were doing but the great majority proceeded out of simple obedience to authority.

Dr. Milgram later wrote: "With numbing regularity, good people were seen to knuckle under the demands of authority and perform actions that were callous and severe. Men who were in everyday life responsible and decent were seduced by the trappings of authority...into performing harsh acts." He drew this conclusion about the general population outside the experimental theatre: "A substantial proportion of the people do what they are told to do, irrespective of the content of the act and without limitations of conscience, so long as they perceive that the command comes from a legitimate authority."

He might also have observed that the New Haven people who got up and walked out when severe voltages were ordered knew they faced no sanctions once outside that room. They returned to a safe and quiet world, not to a concentration camp or an executioner.

I met and spent an afternoon once with a former SS concentration camp guard, a big, lonely, haunted man who lived on the Alaska Highway. How he got into Canada, despite the war crime, and whether he was ever driven out of Canada I do not know. I remember his story well. He was a Ukrainian, one of the half million Red Army men captured by the Germans in the first months of their Russian campaign, herded into camps and left to starve to death. There was more of him to starve; he was two metres high. When prison camp starvation was well advanced and men were beginning to eat each other he joined the Ukrainian SS Division and came out of the war alive instead of dead. This for the benefit of those who wish to judge him but haven't been faced with death by starvation. It might help their understanding of things.

The Milgram experiment stands, to reproach us all. The death camp SS guards and Ukrainian deserters were people like you and I. This was one of the more shocking aspects of the Nazi death camp story. The guards and commandants were among the cruellest human beings imaginable. What can be said for guards who laughed while little children were being torn away from their mothers to be machine-gunned or, in the later refinements, thrown into the gas ovens? Yet in the following decades, when these unutterably savage men were discovered, they turned out to be pretty much like men anywhere. They had houses in the suburbs, they fretted about mortgage payments and straightening their daughters' teeth, they watched TV, drank beer and sang good songs at parties.

The experiment which showed that ordinary people have the capacity to run death factories has been repeated, under controlled conditions, several times since, despite the protests of those who say that academic freedom does not license anybody to encourage depravity in citizens and, worse, come up with unpalatable findings. Reports of the experiment were pretty successfully buried by the year 2000 but those of us who studied the results twenty years before could not forget them, although we would have preferred to.

Like most Canadians, I had a good war, safe at home. Rheumatic fever took me out of the RCAF before I got to England, where our bomber crews were then running 25 percent losses in a single tour of duty. The war produced prosperity at home and the deaths, troubling though they were, didn't mean that much to a people used to the carnage on the highways.

Having seen no war, I have personally seen no massive suffering and cruelty and am grateful. I don't permit myself the illusion that it cannot happen here and, though I regret saying it, my neighbours and I in sunny Canadian suburbia have the same capacity to breed men to operate the gas chambers of a concentration camp and women to make lampshades out of the victims' skins.

It happened a little more easily in Germany in the 1930s and '40s than it would here because the Germans, by unfortunate impulse, had chosen a criminal gang to be their rulers with a lunatic as their leader. When it is the policy of a government to loose the worst instincts in men, the horrors that result are a natural outcome. There was also the lamentable German characteristic, centuries old, of submitting to authority. "We take entire responsibility for this. Please do not stop, you will spoil the experiment."

That it happened more easily there should not cloud the truth that the Nazis drew upon two factors of our makeup, the herd instinct and the natural sin born into man and baboon.

Any who doubt can find it in children, who, most of the time, are the creatures who brighten our lives and make the whole thing seem worthwhile. Never forget the child's natural capacity for cruelty. Few parents have watched their children grow to adulthood without witnessing spasms of vile, cruel and bestial behaviour toward other children, almost always weaker ones. Almost always children behave this way when in a group rather than alone. A few parents must bear the anguish of seeing their children grow to adulthood and never lose the psychopathic impulses that come and go while growing up. In all of us, civilization is something we have to be taught, with occasional refresher courses as we go through life.

Time Surprises Old Father William

IN THE YEAR 2002 when the German shorthair and I went out for quail, I carried an aluminum three-legged stool at my belt. Every thirty or forty minutes I would unfold the stool, sit and ponder what vast cosmic plan is served by sciatica. Sometimes while pondering I would rock back and forth on the three legs a bit and nod off for a minute or two. Who would have thought I should come to this or, if I did come, so soon. As the first Elizabethans used to say with that wondrous turn of phrase they had, "Time doth surprise us all." In the reign of the second Elizabeth my great-aunt Jennie put it differently: "Old age is a tragedy."

You get clumsy; things are nearer or farther away than you think. When you find old school friends you haven't seen for years, you discover they have turned into old farts. Other people don't speak loudly and clearly the way they used to and you are surprised by the fact policemen nowadays are just kids. It does make you wonder if getting into the movies for a dollar is enough to compensate.

Even the youngest of my descendants who read these words will, in their turn, be surprised by time. That is, they will unless accident or ill health snatch them early, or their society requires euthanasia of people before sciatica and other signs of age begin to show. The Japanese apply euthanasia thinking to mechanical creations and do not permit people to keep and drive old automobiles; in many parts of North America we have taken our first steps toward getting rid of the old early by denying driver's licences to people solely on the basis of birthday counts.

At present, in Japan and predominantly in European nations, many people are stringing along until they reach the century mark, much to the distress of companies who sold them annuities in good faith, not anticipating that medical science was going to interfere and cause the customers to live long and ruin the profit projections. We all have our own troubles.

However, I am in the grip of the Protestant work ethic, from which I have often tried to escape and failed. It tells me that all man's waking hours should be put to some productive purpose, otherwise God or some other omnipotent force will punish me. So I keep hunting. The quail, of course, may hold a different point of view, although I can report that most of them don't seem to care.

Honesty compels me to say that I am immensely grateful to all the other people who have the work ethic and insist it is better to wear out than to rust out. Western and Japanese societies, and more recently due to industrialization the Chinese people, have created a marvellous world of good health and creature comforts. We live immensely better than ever before and not many of us spoil it by getting severe attacks of religion. In our post-industrial world there remain no truly poor people, the families of alcoholics and a few other unfortunates being the rare exceptions. It's trite but true that Solomon in all his glory knew no life as good as is the average man's today. Solomon? Forget Solomon, Midas, the Sun King and other historic figures. The world's mightiest and wealthiest of a mere fifty years ago did not have the service, the comfort or the opportunity for intellectual stimulation that is every man's lot in the new millennium.

For decades, western man has watched yesterday's luxury become today's necessity, and although the currency has been debased by almost every government, even cheap currency buys more than was imaginable the day before yesterday. Beside me on the desk as I write this is an alarm clock. Fifty odd years ago I bought my first windup alarm clock. I could only afford a second-hand one; they were expensive. I would have spared myself even that cost except for the danger of losing my job by sleeping in. It kept time more or less, when you remembered to wind it. This digital alarm clock of today, accurate to within a second or two a month, with a bell that never fails to ring when set, cost me one Canadian dollar, which would be sixty-five American cents. How can a dollar buy so much? People had to make the chip that governs it, assemble this clock and put a maple leaf on the face, then ship it 4,000 to 10,000 miles to market, and pay duty on it when entering the country. In addition to import duty, there had to be a profit for a manufacturer, a jobber, a wholesaler, a shipper and a retailer. How long will it be, I wonder, before the Chinese pay me money to take alarm clocks off their hands?

Respecting this highly productive Protestant work ethic — respecting far more than liking — I shall continue in it for my lifetime and in the sweat-and-strive spirit I try now to tell young people unborn about aging. This is the one fundamental difference that will always maintain a separation between generations, the fact that everybody now old was once young but nobody now young has ever been old, not even me in my sober childhood. I must hope that the habits of a lifetime devoted to the ideal of objective prose will keep me from tumbling into the pedantry of Southey's "You are old, Father William..." If not, too bad.

Aging is not all that awful, provided it doesn't go on too long. It seems just wonderful when you think of the alternative. Some things, like sciatica, are unappealing and seem pretty damn pointless also. The relentless decline of sexual powers is bothersome to all, particularly men, who must experience the stages of "triweekly, try weekly, try weakly." Older women are more likely to find the situation amusing or even agreeable and go shopping, as noted in an earlier chapter. The spectre that haunts us all is Alzheimer's disease, which can eventually remove us even from the animal kingdom so that we become mere vegetables. I have suicide arrangements for that possibility and pray that our society will before too long have the elementary decency to show to humans the mercy that animal shelters give to dying dogs. Man has a particular talent for cruelty toward his own kind.

Even if we don't become prey to Alzheimer's, our brains, which for a lifetime quenched most of our memories so we were not driven mad by sensory overloads, now carry that therapeutic process to extremes. We discard information too readily and after a while we can't be left to supervise the grandchildren any more. It's too bad, but the aging brain clears away too much clutter, and pieces of the family silver get swept up with the wrapping paper and go out into the garbage. I keep in my office a wooden plaque, bought in Prince Edward Island at the Anne of Green Gables store, appealing, in part, because it is about age yet discovered in a shrine of youth. It reads: "I love my bifocals / My dentures fit fine / My hearing aid's perfect / But, Lord, I miss my mind."

The short-term memory becomes increasingly fallible with age. I can remember the kids who came to my sixth birthday party but I don't know where I left the car keys. However, in some respects, memory is improved; we learn to not bother remembering a few things that weren't worth finding out in the first place.

And there are compensations, beyond the compensations of mere wisdoms that I talk so much about. At its best, old age is the gloaming of man's day, a rather beautiful time when the winds cease, the day's toil ends and the angelus sounds to remind us of eternity. One of the things that happen every day at evening is an alteration to the human vision system. Scientists call it the Purkinje Effect for the man who first studied it in some detail. Unlettered fishermen in a Mexican village will call it the Blind Time because they know it is a dangerous period of vision alteration when accidents often occur. The physical alteration to the human eye that takes place at dusk is an evolutionary adaptation, developed in the days when we were small, weak mammals in a large, cruel world. We needed both day and night vision to avoid being eaten. In daylight, the cones of the eye are drawn forward. They are precise and they recognize colour. Thus we are better able to see the tiger hidden in the reeds and we can also tell the ripe red berries from the unpalatable green ones.

In the gloaming, the cones retreat into the eyeball and the rods come forward. The rods are for black and white vision. They do not see as precisely as do the cones but they are quick to pick up peripheral movement, which is what saved so many of our ancestors from a leopard's leap during the nights. The eye is the last body organ to fully develop and the Purkinje Effect is one reason that teenagers, who still have underdeveloped eyeballs and poor peripheral vision, have so many auto accidents involving vehicles coming at them from the side. The changeover time is particularly tricky because the eyes develop complete temporary blind spots in front. The experienced motorist tries to avoid driving during this dangerous period of time. If he must, experience teaches him to turn his head slightly to one side, enabling his peripheral vision to take over from the cone/colour vision at the front of the eye, which is shutting down.

The parallel of the Purkinje Effect and the aging mind is not exact, few parallels are, but there is a similar process in the old person's mind at life's twilight. Our perspective alters. The world has not altered around us, but we see it differently.

One example: The spike buck says, "Look at all those does over there, let's run over and screw a couple of them." The old buck says, "Let's walk over and screw them all." There are, however, more worthy observations to be made from the vantage point of age and experience.

There is that small but hurtful little matter of the humiliation you suffer when you make a fool of yourself. It happens in school, beginning in kindergarten, on the playing fields, in the home, at work and, above all else, in the pursuit of love. These are not mere gaucheries, they are acts or words that put your genuine weaknesses and failings on public display. I can feel the sting of a few such occasions from twenty, thirty and forty years ago. Occasionally they are absurd enough to be comic, even to yourself, but more often they appall your auditors and, sooner or later, yourself. Animals also, particularly the domestic dog, are hurt and dismayed when they make themselves look foolish. Dog owners know this and you may notice that when a dog does something ungraceful and silly, if he is an old dog with white on the muzzle and cloudy eyes, the owner usually won't laugh at him but will give him a friendly pat.

I probably managed to live with the memories of self-inflicted humiliations as well as the average person, but for some, making himself a fool had lifelong consequences. We all have our sensitivities but some, usually people called shy, are more easily damaged than others. I would like to help any who read this and recognize themselves as having been damaged by their own vain, egotistical, silly or stupid words on one occasion or another. For your good health, there are several things for you to remember and the most important is the simplest and often the last recognized: everybody makes a fool of himself now and then. There are no exceptions to this rule among people of ordinary character and intelligence. None. Not one exception. The second is that those who witness your humiliating foolishness are much more interested in themselves than in you. They cannot be bothered giving the matter much thought. And if, sometimes, they do, memories also soon fade. Time takes care of most things for us.

Should it be, then, that we learn from our fooleries, take them as lessons for strengthening character? No. Far better to say the hell with it. To dwell upon them is basically selfish, reflecting a feeling that you are not only the centre of everybody's attention but also deserve to be. Shit happens. Forget it.

Instead remember the truly bad things of your life, the occasions when you said things that had no purpose except to hurt another human being's feelings. In later years, those are the occasions you regret above all others. Almost always it is too late to make amends and sometimes amends are impossible at the moment the words are uttered. Those are the times when you joined the chickens in pecking a weakling member of the flock to death. This is the nasty side of human nature and I have been guilty, guilty, guilty as charged. Some people whom I set out to hurt may have deserved it but I can't remember exactly who appointed me to be judge, jury and executioner. I do know those occasions curdle the memory. There were other occasions, more numerous no doubt, when I wasn't aware of the pain I caused; the words were accidentally dropped, the appointment was forgotten, the promise mislaid. Those were crimes without intent but they, too, were crimes against humanity and visible to the eyesight of the later years. Remember Robbie Burns: "Then gently scan your brother man, / Still gentler, sister woman; / Tho' they may gang a kennin wrang, / To step aside is human."

Do these reflections have anything to do with peripheral vision provided us by the rods in our eyes, which warn us that the *Ocean Limited* is coming down the track toward us moving, as big trains do, four times faster than is apparent? Yes, they do.

The Secrets of Success

BEFORE WE SPEAK ABOUT SUCCESS we should first define what it is, because the word means different things to different people. To a two-year-old, it means getting through a day without peeing your pants. To a thirty-year-old, it is making a huge heap of money. To a ninety-year-old, it is getting through a day without peeing your pants.

For the purpose of this chapter I am accepting as the definition of success achievement so large it has impact on the rest of society. This may be making a pile of money, it may be discovering the polio vaccine, it may be building ocean-going freighters at the rate of one per day. It is achievement on a scale the rest of the world could not ignore if it chose to try.

Not being by nature an original thinker, most of my life I unthinkingly accepted the words of German dramatist Johann von Schiller, perhaps echoing Thucydides: "Against stupidity the very gods / Themselves contend in vain." It's a typical comment of a member of the chattering classes, who never see their own faces reflected in the waters of either the well or the cesspool. I accepted it because it was so facile. Intellect, brains, intelligence, savvy—that was a quality that came close to guaranteeing success in this world. The second, allied to it, was education. The good mind, trained, was unbeatable, and people would say of such men that the sun shone out of their asshole.

Before I was 50, I had all the evidence anybody should have needed to prove that this simplistic notion was as false as most simplistic notions are. Being in the newspaper business all those working years, I rubbed shoulders with a good many spectacular successes. There were a few spectacular failures also, thanks be, because crime and catastrophe, not shining successes, are what sell newspapers and buy whisky for the poor suffering scribes of the press.

Wildly successful people, although less newsworthy, were nevertheless objects of curiosity for the inquiring minds we newspapermen are expected to have. I inquired often and learned much about successful people but was never able to take the one step out of the box to see what I had learned. When old enough to know better, I did that and discovered that few if any of the successful men and women were of outstanding intelligence and at least half of them had scant formal education. Of all their qualities, the two I had weighted at 99 percent as a success factor came in at a value more like 20 percent.

How could I have been so wrong? Easy, dear descendants. Just adopt the popular wisdom of your day and you, too, can be wrong for most of a lifetime.

To illustrate my discovery that people get to the top with little of the qualities that popular wisdom declares to be essential, I offer Sarah Bernhardt, perhaps the most famous actress who ever lived. Today we think our society is far gone — much too far gone, many say — in worship of movie queens. Such people forget history. There has never been an actress to arouse such extravagant admiration as The Bernhardt. Not only did theatre audiences unhitch the horses from her carriage and draw her themselves through the cheering crowds — the adoration extended to governments and to aristocrats. The Czar, Autocrat of All the Russians, restrained her from curtseying and instead, in public, bowed to her.

While the ability to act is all very well, it's usually thought that beauty plays a large part in an actress's life. Well, the entire world agreed that Divine Sarah was beautiful, a radiant beauty quite beyond the dreams of ordinary mortals. No doubt she was, but not in physical terms. Photos show otherwise. Also we have the testimony of dispassionate observers. Joseph A. Harriss, writing of her in *Smithsonian Magazine*, reports that her superb acting "compensated for being no great beauty."

Her hair was hopeless, a frizzy, unruly, reddish blond. She hid her low brow below a tumble of curls, which also had the advantage of enlarging her small eyes. And in a day when the canons of beauty called for opulent, Rubenesque women, she was not only thin, she was skeletal. "Madonna's head stuck on a broomstick," as the writer Alexandre Dumas *fils* called her.

So now, in retrospect, I ask what were the qualities that made some people great while others, many of whom had greater competence by any usual standard of measurement, could be good but were invariably recognized to be less than great?

The difference between excellence and greatness is immense. In politics, why is choosing a prime minister so difficult? It is because, until he is there, nobody can know whether he is great. There are no measurements of character worth calibrating in the choice of somebody so important to the general good. We only know that there are many good men who make good and even brilliant first mates but very few who can ever be captains.

Some of the qualities that make for success finally do become apparent. I list them as they come to mind. I may miss one or two but be assured I am generally right in these judgments and know that I am right.

Courage is an essential. So is ambition. So also is self-confidence. Very few who don't believe in themselves can do much with themselves. Integrity is so important that one marvels that our schools and colleges do not teach it, but perhaps it is an unteachable quality. As far as I know, all the successful men I have observed had integrity. Their word was good. Loyalty is another factor for success. The top people were loyal to those around them and in that way fostered a loyalty to themselves.

Enthusiasm matters. I can recall no successful men or women who were not enthusiasts.

Sometimes, although not always, because some great successes were loners all their lives, there existed the magic quality of leadership. We all recognize it when we encounter it but when we try to analyze it we sometimes have difficulty. I turn to Napoleon Bonaparte, the meteor who streaked across the skies of Europe in the eighteenth century, almost succeeding in creating a united European federation, a goal finally reached in my time.

Many have analyzed in detail how Napoleon led an army that was always barefoot and hungry to almost endless victories against the major armies of the continent. The tactics—surprise, speed and concentration of forces—are less important than the quality of his field marshals. Napoleon recognized and rewarded that rare quality of leadership wherever and whenever he found it, and Marshal Ney, who spent his boyhood sweeping horse turds in a stable, defeated the best generals the aristocracies of Europe could send against him. Napoleon himself was defeated, not only at Waterloo but earlier and more significantly in Spain, by a man of the same sort as himself—Arthur Wellesley, non-aristocrat by birth and a natural leader.

Let me take a moment to remember wise words that I and others should have heeded more. In the late '50s, I interviewed Major General Matthew Penhale on his retirement. He was a physically unimpressive man of the nickname "Pearshape Penhale." He is not remembered as well as he should be. The Canadian Army was then commissioning officers in much the same way as the British did in order to arrange their catastrophes in the Crimea with Raglan of the Light Brigade and other titled idiots. Our army was not picking aristocrats, which was good, but we were, we thought, picking brains out of the universities, sparing them the marching, countermarching and short arm inspections and loosing their talents instantly into military affairs.

General Penhale had doubts. An army was a strange organization, he observed. It asked people to please go out and die in the course of their work. Getting men to do this at any time,

Alexander the Great's or today, requires the quality called leadership. It appears here and there and fails to appear elsewhere when expected and needed. Let us welcome the technicians, said the general, but what are we doing to find leadership, without which all else that an army stands for collapses? Leadership emerges; it is not taught as nuclear physics or astronomy is taught. I see now that he was telling me much more than I appreciated. The report I wrote for the *Vancouver Sun* was mundane, casual and instantly forgettable. General Penhale deserved better from me and from his country.

One qualification for success that emerges time and again, so often it must have significance, is the ability of some men and women to exercise intuition. We all have intuition but often fail to use it when we should. Logical left-brain thought has dominated western culture since the Industrial Revolution and only recently has there been some return to the brain's right hemisphere, partly thanks to the radiation pattern normal to television tubes. Where most of us see a problem, the intuitive mind is able to step outside the confines of conventional and rational thought and perceive that it is not a problem at all, it is an opportunity.

Forget people like Alexander the Great. A humdrum example will do. Eventually the script of this book is converted to a paper manuscript and in the editing of it, we frequently use little yellow notes called Post-its. They enable you to find a page or subject easily and, once used, the note can be thrown away, leaving no trace on the paper. These little notes, used all over the world, began as a problem. IBM had been researching a new paper glue that was to have some superior quality or other but the damned stuff wouldn't stick. The problem was handed to a young executive and he was told to come up with a decision. Should more money be spent on research? Should the glue formula be sold off to a competitor for what it would bring? Should the whole project be abandoned and the losses written off now rather than later when they would be bigger? That man had the ability to step outside the box. "Let's not keep trying to change the glue," he said. "Let's change the customer. Look for customers who want glue that doesn't stick too well." I hope he enjoys the yacht at Cannes and the ski lodge at Aspen. Mere intelligence and education could not have provided him that success; it was his method of using intelligence that counted.

As for intelligence itself, where did I, your progenitor of the year 2002, fit?

Some may have thought me an intellectual or at least a pseudo-intellectual. They were wrong on the second count—I never wanted to join the chatterers—and probably wrong on the first also, because I lacked the explorative mind. I was probably well above average in intelligence tests. There were no IQ tests when I was young, or none I knew about, but if I had taken one I would probably have scored well, given my training in standards of WASP society. In school I was known as what would today be called a nerd—bookish, silent, solitary but able to put the right answers in the right boxes at examination time.

My mother, God bless her, did her best to keep me flying straight, wings beating, no gliding. She told me one day, "People say you are very intelligent, but you are not. What you have is a phenomenal memory. You can be told something just once and play it back instantly. However, you have no original thoughts." From time to time she also used to call me "Canada's youngest little old man." Those words stuck, as did others such as "I don't care what you are in life—tinker, soldier, sailor, spy—just be good at it." In old age she used to deny saying the last, but she did. I remember.

This may make my mother seem a cold and insensitive woman, a judgment that might be supported by the fact she often repeated that when I was a little kid and hurt myself she would forbid me to cry. But she was not cold or insensitive and she loved me to distraction, as I loved her. I have always been grateful that in the 1920s and '30s she was not among those scavenging scraps of humbug scattered about by that old Viennese mountebank, Sigmund Freud. She knew that, like most kids, I didn't bruise easily. Much more important, she paid me the high honour of believing that I had the moral fibre to hear unwelcome truths about myself spoken loud and clear.

Like many people of such wisdom, she probably seemed unworldly to many. Certainly she was not one of the chattering classes and never wanted to join them. She said, on another occasion, "I thank God that He never made me sophisticated. I have been able to get so much more enjoyment out of life."

To my descendants I say, this is a female ancestor who deserves to be a bright star on your family tree. She had a beautiful soul and common sense too. Whether she made a success of me, I don't know. Probably a bit, here and there. But it doesn't seem to matter much now, although it is politically incorrect for me to say so in a world where nothing else is thought to be worth a tinker's dam.

More important, I say this across the years that separate us. Success is an odd thing, not necessarily satisfying and usually a secret known only within your own heart. Some don't want it and others achieve it and never recognize it. But if you wish to pursue it, my experience tells me that courage, confidence, integrity and other qualities that are often considered peripheral may instead be central and crucial, far more important than the calibre of your artillery pieces.

Verities and Mysteries

Faith in Fuzzy Quantums

WHEN I WAS YOUNG and the planet was still cooling down, my trust in science was almost limitless. That has never changed much. Now, as then, I was contemptuous of priests, with all those stories that they borrowed from just about all the other priests of all the other religions in the Middle East. There is too much in Christianity that the commonest of common sense rejects. Organized religion may have been a natural development in the days when we couldn't read or write and didn't even know what caused thunderstorms or appendicitis, but the necromancy persisted far too long in a world that could and should be at least mildly rational.

Priesthoods have always known this and resisted the advance of scientific knowledge. The popes recognized early that if the world went around the sun, some of the faithful were bound to wonder how Joshua could stop it spinning one day as he pursued some genocidal mission for the greater glory of his God. All of the churches knew that many of their legends would not withstand Darwin's book about the origin of the species. Their first response was denial, the second was persecution of those who brought forward evidence of the real world. The Roman Catholic Church doesn't burn people at the stake any more for teaching the facts about the solar system, and even the Southern Baptists, sometimes called Methodists who can't read, have accustomed themselves to the thought that the universe may indeed be more than a few thousand years old. However, if my progeny can read these words a century from now they may not realize how many people at this time, in a comparatively well educated society, clung to beliefs that were not only absurd but dangerously so.

In the year 2001, seven percent of the people answering a public opinion poll said they would commit murder if they believed that their ever-loving and merciful God told them to do so, as he told Abraham to kill his son. Do you know twenty people? Consider that if this survey is accurate, one of them is prepared to kill you if, like Joan of Arc, he suffers from a disorder in the left temporal lobe of the brain that can cause people to think they hear voices. Joan's case turned out better than some. Her condition improved. Research indicates it was another ditsy girl who was burned at the stake in Rouen. Joan went on to get married in the usual way and raised kids, the famed Charles de Gaulle being among her descendants. However, the dingbat who hears voices about you, if she be among those seven out of every hundred people, may keep the true faith by murdering you in obedience to God's will, just as many loving parents killed their kids in the Jones colony. Faith can be very dangerous material to handle.

For all these complaints about religion, I have seldom met a priest I didn't like. (For priest read pastor, elder, rabbi or one of the other names that some churches prefer to call their priests.) Yes, there were a few I disliked. One, I remember, was a supporter of the Croatian Ustashe regime of the Second World War, a government so foul that not even the Nazis would recognize it and the Vatican was the only state on earth willing to exchange ambassadors with it. The smell of evil lay darkly about that man. There have been one or two others. But almost all I have encountered, professionally or socially, were men who gave up some creature comforts of this world to pursue an ideal, surely an admirable thing. For that alone, they deserve the respect of most men. Most of them were appealing human beings. I sometimes wonder if perhaps I would have found some of the same charm in Grand Inquisitor Tomás de Torquemada; in Cardinal Spellman of Boston, who, in support of Vietnam's Christians, promoted the American invasion of that country with all its attendant horrors; or in fundamentalist Ian Paisley, who, more than any other one man, set the Northern Irish to killing each other in the second half of the last century. These were predominantly evil men but there were perhaps gleams of a pure white light amid the murk of their souls.

Now, pray tell, how much better is science?

The scientists also preach the impossible. Why, if I fly to the stars at speeds approaching that of light, will I return still a young man while my entire generation will have died centuries before? How can I even now become chronologically older than people on the ground by going around and around the earth in a satellite, or even sitting on a mountaintop, where time is infinitesimally but also measurably slower relative to time on earth's surface? Time was supposed to be time, unalterable as God himself. Now we know that it is not. This is a truth I can repeat, like a catechism, but I cannot comprehend it. But then, I also don't comprehend what a billion is, a figure now in everyday use. You don't know what it is either, although you may think you do. We can all do the arithmetic and produce figures for billions and for trillions and quadrillions and add, subtract and multiply them. But the poor human mind can't do much more than play with those figures on paper or on a backlit phosphor screen. We do not have the capacity to visualize billions as we do figures such as five, eight and a dozen, which, for almost the entire age of the human race, were all we needed. For most of our existence we didn't need to count better than the average crow, which counts one, two, three, four, five and then many. Maybe, just maybe, we can manage figures as high as a thousand today but the rest are pure leaps of faith in mathematics.

This applies to a broad spectrum of scientific knowledge. We know from the evidence of our senses that the world is flat but we accept the proofs of the scientists that it is not. Modern science has pretty well convinced us that very few things obvious are true—those railway tracks don't really come together as they near the horizon—and also that many things improbable or impossible are likely to exist.

Why should we accept the fuzzy quantum on faith but not the story of Jonah living in the whale's digestive juices or that God abhorred people who ate meat on Fridays until the 1960s, at which time he changed his mind and left all the imps of hell confused about how to treat the souls who had been Friday roast beef people?

There are a couple of pretty good reasons to trust scientists. One is that they don't burn us to death in the town square at noon because we failed to believe something they dreamed up. Scientists, in fact, welcome skepticism. The other, better reason is that when challenged to prove their theories, scientists almost always can do so while religionists invariably retreat to cant, appeal to the magic quality of faith or, sometimes, resort to wild rage.

So I am not unhappy that I cannot understand that gravity is a curvature of space-time and that quantum mechanics impose fuzziness on ripples in space-time from 15 billion years ago. As far as my brain capacity allows me to follow processes, the proof of scientific discovery is always there to be found. When scientists extend their thinking farther than I can follow, as does that grotesquely physically handicapped resident genius of our age, Stephen Hawking, who develops theories reaching into God's own private garden, they are believable even if not understandable.

And Mr. Hawking does not demand belief or obedience from me. That is much to be preferred over Catholic and Protestant priesthoods who explicitly or implicitly accept the words attributed to Christ, "No man comes to the Father except through me." Otherwise expressed as "Do it my way or go to hell." Modesty was not a characteristic of the Saviour depicted in the Bible.

I speak lightly of things that are heavy. That is what is good about these times. You may speak lightly about religion and occasionally be called the Antichrist, but who cares any more? As for speaking lightly about science, that qualifies you as a skeptic and you can expect to be at least more acceptable than the neighbourhood tomcat.

The most important statement of my lifetime is this one: "Ninety-eight percent of all the scientists who ever lived are alive today." It may not be quite as important as the Sermon on the Mount but at present its effects are dazzlingly evident everywhere we look. The century 1900–2000 was the Big Bang in the creation of a new intellectual universe. If, one hundred years from now, it will be said that the year 2000 was the mere beginning of scientific advance, I would not be in the least surprised, were I around to hear it. I know only that almost all the *Arabian Nights* stories have come true during my lifetime—flying carpets, genies in bottles and all the rest.

I offer in evidence no more than a few of this particular month's science and technology news items: The first modern computer occupied two floors of a large warehouse in Washington after the Second World War. Computers are soon going to be built small enough to be inserted in our arteries so they may travel through the body reporting on health conditions. This week scientists at Brown University on Rhode Island reported implanting dime-sized electrodes in the brains of three Rhesus monkeys, which, thereafter, were able to play pinball games using the power of their thoughts only, with no physical manipulation of the machines. This is clearly a good, long step toward the Microsoft boffin's forecast that before long we'll be able to learn foreign languages, nuclear physics or Immanuel Kant's philosophy by having a chip implanted under our skin, with regular upgrades available.

Another report states that what has long been considered the ultimate truth, that light moves at the fastest possible speed and that to go faster than light would reverse time, is now being questioned, and there is a scientific paper that claims that what the science fiction writers call warp speed, faster than light speed, has been achieved for a millisecond or so by Russian researchers. It is another thing that minds such as mine cannot digest. Also I really don't want to be my own grandfather someday, but warp speed is at least thinkable in this age.

Another advance was made this month in the creation of designer children. With the aid of science, some parents have selected the sex of children to whom they wish to permit birth. A lesbian couple who are totally deaf demanded court approval of their plan to have one of them bear a totally deaf child for their home. In the natural course of events we may expect fads about child types to wax and wane, with people choosing tall, short, blue-eyed, brown-eyed offspring. I detest the idea of interfering in childbirth in this way, ending mankind's greatest of all the lotteries, but the knowledge is now there—the genie is out of his bottle and cannot be stuffed back in.

I speak as one whose knowledge of science and technology never advanced much beyond understanding the whistling tea kettle. Strangely—I didn't expect it in myself—I have almost no interest in finding out how most miracles are accomplished by the scientists and technicians. Earlier in the technologic age, the '50s, I was different. I learned to rebuild automobile engines as a sideline pursuit, understood porting and polishing of racing engines and knew the virtues of the square and oversquare engine, which today even the sellers of square engines usually do not know. I had, in fact, progressed well beyond the whistling kettle. Perhaps it was a phase, which is what we used to say about our teenage children's behaviours. In any case, the curiosity that once existed is gone from me. There are more people like me out here than the manufacturers of computers can imagine. Most of us really don't care about the details. We would be quite content if told that our personal computers are operated by some unusually adept little white mice who live inside the machine and exist on the crumbs we drop through the keyboard from our jalapeño-flavoured potato chips.

There is one thing that all true scientists seem to have always known but the rest of us didn't—how little scientists do know.

Isaac Newton, a genius of his age, compared his discoveries with somebody picking up a pebble on a beach beside an almost limitless ocean. Every discovery brings us not to the end of some search but to the beginnings of a larger search. Questions continue to be created faster than answers.

One of the areas in which immense discoveries were made in the last two decades of the millennium was the human brain, an organism of staggering complexity. We are born with a hundred billion brain cells (another of those confusing billion figures) and, according to whatever expert you consult, we use 1 to 20 percent of them. The capacity of this lump of greasy grey material that we are only now beginning to understand is so vast as to challenge the act of description. Is it enough to say that the total number of electrical connections within your brain network numbers more than the entire number of particles in the entire universe?

Sexual variations in the brain are considerable. Men vary more in intelligence between highs and lows and there seems to be a greater separation of the right and left hemispheres. More men are in the arts, the sciences and the mental institutions. Boys are more curious, more impulsive and more easily distracted. Girls have more highly developed language skills, process information faster than boys and are better at remembering names, faces, odours, tastes and touch sensations.

This is not the time or place to explore those questions—in any case, today's answers are likely to be toppled tomorrow—but brain research does deserve some special attention by us all for what it has already taught us about the importance of laughter in human affairs, the virtues of gut feelings and intuitions over the calm, cool and rational behaviour that was long urged upon us and, finally, at least a peek at the great mystery of art. After all, the cave paintings and all the art that followed had not the slightest direct advantage as survival mechanisms. They kept no sabre-toothed tigers at bay, they offered no improvement of diet or domicile. Then and now they served some higher purpose. We sometimes call that purpose civilization, but that is a poor word; there was no civilization when the first cave paintings were done.

Finally, we are beginning to talk about travelling not to the planets but to the stars, and if another few centuries must pass before that happens, we have at least and at last given up the absurd notion that our planet is the only speck in the cosmos that nourishes intelligent life.

Out of it all emerges the main question. Are we better or worse people today for the Big Bang of knowledge?

It's strange but true that we have learned an immense amount about how, but we still don't know any more about why.

In terms of health and wealth all humanity is immensely better off, but probably we are worse people. Our souls have suffered. Science, which has no soul, submerged our religious impulses, which were the best police force any society had ever developed. Science usually tended to denigrate intuition and the arts and induce the belief that only the material aspects of life mattered. But is this important? Science is not a way of life, it is not a creed nor, properly, is it a faith. It is a tool, to be used for better or worse. When the *Titanic* hit an iceberg and sank, did anyone complain that the iceberg lacked a soul? What happened was that we began iceberg patrols in the North Atlantic, which scientists had made possible, but knowing all the while that there will be more collisions with bergs. The collision and our reaction were all part of the mighty river of events on which we are carried, with its whirlpools, its rapids and its calm and still waters where the lilies float, the river we call history.

The Mad, Glad Impulse

When I drive across a bridge I always calculate my chances of surviving if it collapses. At first approach, the odds are good because the drop to the solid ground beneath isn't much worse than a tumble down a steep bank. Farther out, it's a long way to the hard ground and my chances lessen. But then they get better again over the water. People jump off very high bridges and survive. In the cushioned upholstery of an automobile the jolt should be even easier to take, although the question of getting out of the sinking car remains. Then I'm over land again and high risk decreases to zero as I leave the bridge pavement and join the street system. A similar serpent of thought glides through my mind in tunnels. Can you come up with a more useless bit of thought?

If it helps to understand my little phobia—it has never helped me but I offer the information anyway—I have never avoided using a bridge because it might collapse. That includes using some old, condemned wooden bridges in the Chilcotin Country that might actually have fallen down under me. More than once I drove around barricades to get onto creaking old timbers and take a shortcut to some trout pool. Once I was on a major bridge during an earthquake. It was the Burrard Bridge in Vancouver. One of that region's familiar little tremors had rattled a few teacups in the city. The tremor had no effect, one way or the other, on my fear of bridges for the good reason that I have no genuine fear of bridges. I have a neurosis. Over the decades it has just wasted a lot of time I could have used for thinking about making money, drinking rum or something else worth thought. This is offered as one more proof that ordinary good sense is frequently not to be found in the human mind.

The human mind is an ocean of marvels on whose shore we stand and, occasionally, paddle out into the water but without getting to swimming depth. The computer, technology's supreme marvel so far, is merely a monstrous, cretinous adding machine that, at the very most and even then disputably, can attain the intelligence level of a month-old child. Yet in our great brains, which set us apart not only from computers but from the entire animal world, the functions are not only ill understood but also very often not in our own best interests. Some of us are very late in learning this simple fact. Impulse governs much of what we do. The question is, should impulse be suppressed or encouraged to do more?

Impulse is the thoughtless urge. It sends little boys chasing a ball under the wheels of a truck. It creates marriages made for hell. It makes alcoholics and addictive gamblers. The number of battles lost through impulsive behaviour almost equals the number of battles fought. It is flight, sometimes despairing flight, from rational thought. It is also, somehow, a lovely thing, and some of my greatest regrets are for impulses I succeeded in resisting. Perhaps I had an insufficiently misspent youth.

Now how, pray, can I speak of regrets for impulses suppressed? Without doubt, although I cannot remember it, among the impulses I have suppressed was an impulse to run out under the wheels of a truck when I was a kid. Should I regret that? Other impulses come up with memory's tickling, impulses to speak the fatal words that can no more be recalled than an arrow, once loosed, can be brought back to the bow, words that can destroy the friendships of a lifetime, impulses to destroy human relationships with words of righteous anger that, later information showed, were based on totally false premises. There have been impulses to stealing, adultery and a dozen other wrongful things that were suppressed. Surely, then, every impulse should be resisted? Surely we should never act until rational thought has given us the green light? The answer to these questions is no. Impulse can be good for you and impulses quenched can be regretted.

I have great difficulty recalling disastrous impulses that almost overcame my reason, which is why I suspect there weren't many. The others, which I remember better and sadly, are the good impulses I resisted.

I remember a withered crisp of an old gypsy woman, crouched in an alley in Belgrade over a heap of rags she had been collecting. As if it were last night, I remember the impulse to give her money. On that dark night when the cold wind of a new Balkan winter came moaning down on that old city from the Karst, I had much more of the newspaper's expense money in my wallet than I needed and I hadn't been spending much of my own money either. I had been living a few days at well below the standard rate of my account. I could have done the princely thing and given her the equivalent of three hundred Canadian dollars, a lot of money even to me at that time but to her, in dinars, a fortune.

She would have been terrified, seeing some sort of a trap being set for her, but I would do it very swiftly. I would merely walk down the alley, pause a half second, lay the bundle of dinars beside her bundle of rags and walk on, quickly, never to see her again. I would never know what she did with the money but I would always know that the old woman's life, the bit that was left to her, would have been significantly altered, if only for the biggest family party in many years.

I took two steps down the dark and narrow alley. She never looked up. She was as still as somebody who had been stood against a wall and shot down into a bundle of rags. Then all my rational and sensible thoughts took over. I was bewitched, I was foolish. The impulse was smothered at birth. Three hundred dollars was a lot of money, even if part of it belonged to my newspaper.

Forty years later, I know how cheaply I could have bought my own place in the *Arabian Nights*.

An able fiction writer whose name I cannot find wrote a story, long years ago, called "Lee Chong's Million." It was a short story of a US air force pilot visiting Chungking during the Second

World War. For sport, as much as anything, he engaged in bargaining with two Chinese merchants who had a fur jacket to sell. The workmanship, he said, was terrible. "Look at the stitching. See the wrinkled lining." It was just the usual game of bargaining. Then he looked at the twelve-year-old boy who sat at the back of the dingy little store and saw in his eyes that this boy had stitched the jacket together and that he would probably be beaten for what was being said about it.

Later he made it his business to learn the boy's name, Lee Chong. He made arrangements to draw against his air force pay so he could give the youngster a million Chinese yen. But the impulse, like so many, died and little Lee Chong never got his million.

I think of another lost impulse, a harder memory. As a member of the British Columbia Police Commission, I was one of a final court of appeal for citizens or police officers who felt they had not been dealt with fairly under terms of the Police Act. We reviewed the case of a young policeman who had picked up a briefcase with marijuana and cocaine in it and returned to the station with only cocaine. He had been set up and the Vancouver Police Department gladly charged him and dismissed him for lying after he said that the briefcase contained only cocaine.

The real charge against that young man was that he had a brother reputed to be in the drug trade. The department wanted to get rid of him and did. They did it clumsily. With hundreds of millions of dollars worth of illegal narcotics in their possession, they used quantities so small that the only real temptation offered was for him to throw some of it on the street as being too small to bother reporting. A hundred policemen had done the same, being common sense men following the old legal dictum that the law does not concern itself with trivialities. One of our jobs was to hear appeals from police board decisions in police disciplinary matters. Hearing the case reviewed, my conviction grew that the police force should be reprimanded for conducting a kangaroo court. I was going to oppose the dismissal. For support, I referred my ideas privately to a man who knew immensely more law than I knew or could ever know. "You have to find him guilty," he said. "How can a police force operate if its members lie?"

The voice of an expert. I should have remembered one of President John F. Kennedy's few good, original sayings, made after the Bay of Pigs disaster: "All my life I've known better than to depend on the experts. How could I have been so stupid, to let them go ahead?"

I agonized and I reviewed it all a dozen times. Another truism: study any idea long enough and hard enough and you are bound to find more reasons for not doing something than for doing it.

My impulse came back again, late, at the instant of the proclamation of our decision. We were a two-man commission at that time—the government had forgotten to appoint a third commissioner and was in the process of castrating those who remained. I knew what the chairman's decision would be. He was a large, genial civil servant who used to lecture at colleges on bureaucratic process. He had one peculiarity. His right hand was not composed of fingers, thumb and palm but of a rubber stamp, and whenever he heard the word *policy* uttered he would pound this hand into an ink pad and stamp any piece of paper in front of him. It wasn't his fault. He was only a bureaucrat. I was of the public, uninked, and I had every reason to know better.

When he approved the city police board's decision to fire, my impulse flared. I almost said, "I disagree. This is a travesty of justice. The men who arranged this stunt should be on trial." A member's vote was worth only half of a chairman's vote so the dismissal would have stood, but not for long when a proper court of justice examined it.

I did not obey my impulse. I regret it to this day and there is salt in the wound that the young man came up to me after I had betrayed his trust in the name of rational thought. He said he appreciated the care and attention his case had been given.

My impulse of course was as right as the mindless rubber stamp from the commission chairman was wrong. His appointment had violated the principle behind the police commission's formation, which was that a citizen body should act as an advisor on police affairs separate from the bureaucracy. But by that time in my term of office I had learned from a departmental legal advisor called "Sleepy Dick," who always fell asleep during conferences, that most things done by governments at all levels are frequently done without statutory authority and are reversed only if somebody challenges the acts. Governments, like you or I, are not notable law-abiders.

This drags this discussion over to a murky area in which we are asked to define what is legal, what is illegal and, much more important, whether things done illegally should be acknowledged or just quietly done. It's another subject for another page where my despair about the Age of Law making us all, citizens or rulers, act illegally every day is discussed. I will avoid that dismal matter here and confine myself to the subject of impulse.

One fact is clear, that we admire rationality but we love impulse. We love, above all, the impulsive child. We cannot find it in ourselves to be angry enough with the little girl who runs the hose through the window of the family car to see if she can fill it. Something tells us it was an impulse, like a tornado that touches ground only occasionally and randomly, and that it has a kind of magnificence to it. As parents who suffer from such impulses, we may remind ourselves of autistic children who, because of a failure of brain development, seem to be without the quality of human impulse and emotion but remain imprisoned in their own particular cage of rationality.

From where I stand now, I would not want to live in a world where impulse replaced rational thought, but looking at some of the horrors rational thought has produced between the years 1800 and 2000, I am not all that sure that it should be as dominant as we have permitted it to become. If rational thought was right, why should we so love the impulsive people? Should you obey the mad, glad impulse, at least sometimes?

This book is not written to help my great-grandchildren become better people. They will have to figure out right and wrong for themselves. However, I am certain they will all be asked the same riddle about logic and rationality. The only rule I can suggest is that if the impulse is recognizably selfish, resist it. But the fundamental truth about what part impulse should take in the grand scheme of things is something we must grope for. Let us at least ask the question whether western man has fought his own nature too hard in the past couple of centuries. Our institutions, our livelihoods, our day-to-day existence is dominated by left-brain thinking and has been ever since the Industrial Revolution succeeded, if it was a success. Perhaps the truth is we would prefer to follow our instincts more than we do. They may lead us into pain and sufferings but they can lead us also into that condition the French call joy of living.

Is it that we were made for foolish love and fun and lots of make-believe games, that we are not here to be efficient because efficiency is for machines? If I find the answer, I will let you know. I plan another of these books when I hit 95 and then another twenty years later.

Secrets, Codes, Computers and Cover-Ass

IN 1933 THOMAS DUFFERIN PATTULLO, a Klondike gold rush veteran, became premier of British Columbia at a time when there was no gold for anybody, just relief camps, hunger and a lot of bloody-mindedness. He led the province through the Depression and out the other side of it and entered the history books as one of Canada's notable premiers. British Columbia has always gone to extremes in choosing political leaders; we get the best and then we get crooks and lunatics. One of them, Amor de Cosmos, came here from Nova Scotia, where he had the name Smith. Nova Scotians have always said that when he left his home province and came here, the intelligence level of both provinces rose.

Duff Pattullo was a man not easily ignored or forgotten. He resigned office rather than seek to keep out the socialists by going into a coalition with the conservatives, a move that he said would kill the Liberal party, as it did, for half a century. He was a thoughtful man and kept himself endlessly entertained by the art of politics, the art of choosing between the unpalatable and the intolerable.

At a private political meeting in a smoke-filled hotel room one night, he sprang one of his sudden questions on the company. "What is a secret?"

Somebody said, "Something few people know."

"How many know?" he said.

All joined in. Some said ten, some said four or five, a couple said two.

"You are all wrong," said Duff. "A secret is something nobody knows."

What he did not add, but could have, is that once two people do know something, it isn't long before anybody who wants to know has the information. Most people either will not or cannot keep confidential communications confidential. Their promises to do so evaporate with the morning dew. Some betray secrets to make themselves seem important, some do it by malice, a vast number do it carelessly and unintentionally, and even more break secrets as a matter of habit, almost unaware that they break a pledge. In many years of observing people in large and small positions — lawyers, doctors, secret lovers, criminals, politicians, policemen, bureaucrats, wives, husbands and priests — I never ceased to be amazed how freely they exchanged secret information until, at age 70, I realized that a rational man should never reveal something secret unless he fully intends it to be made public sooner or later. Almost all promises to keep secrets and honour confidentiality come with unwritten expiry dates, sometimes tacitly recognized, other times not. The element of time in keeping secrets is completely unpredictable, varying with the people involved. A prudent person will keep in mind the old story of the knight who locked his wife in a chastity belt before leaving for the Crusades. He gave the key to his best friend and told him, should he fail to return within ten years, to unlock the lady then. Before he and his horse were over the horizon he had to stop for his friend, who galloped up behind him shouting, "Wrong key! Wrong key!"

Some of us who are solitary by nature keep secrets longer than other people but there are scarcely any of us truly reliable. Priests hearing confessions seem to be among the best disciples of silence, perhaps because many believe, mistakenly, that there is a law that protects their right of silence. Lawyers can maintain silences well because the law actually does guarantee silence from them on almost all occasions.

Forget laws and customs. They come and they go. What significance can these observations have to a St. Pierre two or three generations down the track?

There are lessons to be learned, I suggest.

One, be a little forgiving. We are in many respects collective creatures, and the impulse to share information is as natural and as innate as our desire to sing, dance and play games together.

Second, perhaps more important in the short view of affairs, realize that to expect any and all governments or large corporations to keep a secret for you is like trying to float a crowbar down a slow creek.

To allow somebody to keep a secret safe for you is to become hostage to his goodwill. In many ways it resembles the signing of treaties by nations. Although most foreign offices are reluctant to put it into words, every treaty your country signs diminishes your sovereign independence. The Americans are among the few nations who keep reminding themselves of this fact and often they deplore it, but the recognition has not prevented them from signing many treaties and vastly diminishing their independence in the world.

Treaties can be good for nations and there are times when you, the individual, will be better off revealing secrets about yourself that you thought it important to hide from the light of day. Just remember what you are doing when you volunteer your secrets to others and pay not the slightest attention to promises that "your secret is safe with us," because it isn't. They'll say it anyway. It is a promise as easy to make as it is to forget.

When I was old enough to know better, I could recall the private information leaked out of the supposedly inviolable records of the income tax department, the revelations of policemen who had no shadow of right to tell me what they knew, the indiscretions of politicians who could have been badly damaged if I hadn't kept quiet for a while, doctors who said what they should not have said about other patients and bankers who revealed other people's strictly private information.

Remember, then, that with every bit of information you pass along to a government or private bureaucracy under promise of confidentiality, you make yourself hostage to them. No matter what they may say, they have little or no feeling of responsibility to adhere to their promise to respect your privacy. If the plane is losing altitude and the mountains are just ahead, your claim to confidentiality is the first bit of excess baggage thrown out to lighten the load.

I speak, so far, only of private information that is made public by carelessness, indifference to terms of a contract or pressure of circumstance. I have not touched upon the large area of technical inability to provide security against invasion of your privacy. In the twenty-first century this may be the most significant privacy issue of all. Not long ago a bright youngster in the Philippines hacked his way into the private files of the huge Ford Motor Company, the Pentagon and the Central Intelligence Agency. He doubtless did it for the same reason that alpinists climb mountains, because they are there. Bless that lad: he's the type to restore our faith in the young generation. His elders in the Philippines may smite him but computer companies will be bidding for his services. He and his like instruct us members of the clumsy multitudes by demonstrating, once again, that we are moving toward a day when clever people with computers will be able to break any code that the mind of man can devise. Unless there is a development today's experts cannot foresee, computers will be incapable of keeping secrets. In the United States the Federal Bureau of Investigation will be able to cease seeking government permission to enter the files of every American citizen because the ability will be such common currency that law could not stand against its reality even if it chose to try.

The protection of your privacy and mine, even now, depends largely upon our unimportance. That is no small protection. Most of us are of little or no importance in either world or local affairs. But it is a chilling thought that private man has been rendered so public a creature. Even today the rulers can, if they choose, be like the fabled grizzly bear who could smell a man a mile downwind and tell the colour of the nightgown his mother wore on her wedding night.

There is more in store for today's people that will be made more visible to tomorrow's people. It is not only private and personal information that has become public, private and personal misinformation about us is abroad and can be even more damaging. It's all too easy to forget the monstrous proportions of bureaucratic inefficiency. In 1995 the CATO Institute investigated United States government databases. The Internal Revenue Service proved to be unreliable 28 percent of the time. The same survey quotes a 1993 study that showed that 369 American income tax bureaucrats in a single regional office had been investigated for browsing records they had no right to observe.

In my personal affairs, I have been paying a Canadian Goods and Services Tax on my earnings since the tax was introduced in 1987. I doubt that a year has passed without that department losing information I sent it. Unlike the income tax department of the Canada Customs and Revenue Agency, which is not only efficient and helpful but also courteous, the shambling GST division is surly and aggressive and, when wrong or confused, its instant reaction is to bluster, bully and threaten legal action. Twice it has threatened me with legal action for failure to pay when, once the dust cleared, it turned out that I had never owed a red cent and that instead the department had been indebted to me.

So know your enemy and fear his inefficiency even more than his malevolence. Your enemy is unlikely to know you or care about you one way or the other but he can wreck your life by error. Which breeds more error. This leads to one of the most damaging features of this age, the practice of cover-ass. In any bureaucracy—public or private makes no difference—once a fault is discovered, the correcting of it is a secondary consideration. The first action is cover-ass. All involved in making the error must quickly demonstrate that not one of them was exactly responsible for anything. "Nobody was driving the car, officer, we were all in the back seat."

Anyone who doubts the extent of cover-ass in the United States or Canada during the '90s should examine the tragic cases of dozens of innocent men who went to jail for life or were executed because of grievous errors and frequent illegal actions by those in authority. In every case, cover-ass came first and justice second, if there was time and the man hadn't been killed by state order. All the cover-ass was successful. Not a single representative of any government apparatus has ever been found responsible for anything in these miscarriages of justice. That includes a woman in Texas who sent several men to the electric chair with scientific testimony she had faked. In Canada and in the US, there has never been a case in which authorities moved with anything other than reluctance and obstruction when scientific tests were needed.

This is not going to change. People in large organizations learn cover-ass as naturally as basketballers learn to dribble, and nobody can enter their heads and remove that knowledge and talent. However, for the common man, it adds greatly to his normal peril at the hands of his rulers.

I suggest these security measures to those who come after me.

Treat any promise of confidentiality by government or private bureaucracies as merely a form of polite social intercourse, such as "I'm pleased to meet you." The confidentiality promise carries no guarantee of performance. You are unlikely to know when confidentiality has been breached and if you should learn of it, you have little or no recourse. That is why I say that the promise bears no more relationship to reality than your insincere response to some stranger to whom you have just been introduced and whom you may or may not be pleased to meet. Always assume that once you provide information it is public information and that your own unimportance is your main defence. A second defence is that we are now swimming in such a tumultuous sea of law and regulation that the rulers cannot summon the money and the energy to enforce most of them. Finally, although bureaucratic inefficiency can kill you, it can also save you; the misinformation about you in the files can be helpful as well as hurtful. Just rid yourself of any notion that a large institution is anxious to correct errors on your records, particularly if they reflect badly upon departmental efficiency. Keep in mind that in these departments are people who have mortgages to meet, cars to repair and children's teeth to be straightened. Walk a mile in their moccasins. Ask where your own main concern would be. They don't even know you and would be more likely to feel an urge to help some old lady across a crowded street.

Remember also that you have some ability to create protective confusions. Big Brother is far more easily confused than most people realize. On the day these words were entered in the laptop the morning news revealed that the itinerary of Queen Elizabeth's tour of Australia had been faxed to a McDonald's restaurant in Sydney, where the manager did know what he was expected to do about it. There are legal moves you can make to help develop such natural confusion. If you have two first names, and most people do, alternate their use on legal documents. It is not against Canadian law, yet, to use your true name on documents, even if you have two true names to use. Remember, your legal rights are far more extensive than either big government or big business wants you to know.

If you are doing things that are unsanctified by either law or political correctness, take measures to avoid leaving a money trail behind you. "Follow the money" is the oldest rule of police investigation. So use common sense. If your restaurant serves Spotted Owl Chowder, don't use your Visa card when you're buying your birds.

Learn a little law. There remain a lot of citizens' rights on the books we inherited from old England, bless her—laws that the new Big Brother state has not yet completely tidied away, although they are kept out of sight. Although the Canadian state is now preparing laws that will monstrously curtail our rights, in the name of battling monstrous terrorists, at time of writing much residual freedom remained within Canada, more than most people knew. Few knew that, except when operating a motor vehicle, they were under no obligation to answer the questions of a police officer who chose to stop them on the street. Few realized there was no such thing as taking a citizen into custody in Canada without making an arrest. Even some of the younger police thought they could take someone into custody for questioning. Not so. They could either arrest or not arrest, and if they arrested they needed reasonable and probable grounds for doing so. Idle suspicion wasn't enough and fishing expeditions were supposedly illegal. How you exercised such rights was a question of time, place and common sense.

Personally, any time a polite policeman wants to talk to me I talk to him. I have not yet lost the conviction that a policeman is on my side—certainly more than the rulers are on my side. He is an ally, not an opponent. But this can change in less than a single generation and some of our rulers are hell-bent on making that change. You are now, for instance, legally obliged to answer a policeman's questions and even to incriminate yourself with your answers if you are politically incorrect about gun ownership.

Also there are other employees of the state who are not so inhibited by law and custom as your friendly local Mountie. A Canada Customs man can oblige you to answer his questions. A US Customs official has the authority to handcuff you and lead you off into the cells if he chooses. Because he found heroin in your bags? No. Nothing like that. He can do it because you said something to him that hurt his feelings. I doubt that King Louis of French Revolution fame had his dignity so diligently protected by law as the people who work in the United States Customs Service.

The ordinary man's privacy, which is another word for secrecy, is diminished monthly, if not weekly, by the actions of the rulers or by their indifference and our own as to whether we lose our rights or not.

At the end of the day, how stands Duff Pattullo's dictum? What he described as a true secret, what nobody knows, is diminished each day by regiments of scientists. Secrecy by the other definition offered by the *Oxford English Dictionary*, the one most of us probably subscribe to, that a secret is something known only to one or a very few people, is being destroyed by the force of law and of technology. Lamentably, the hugely successful terrorist attack on New York's World Trade Center and Washington's Pentagon has given rulers everywhere the excuse for further invasions of privacy. Add to this the human impulse to reveal secrets. Finally comes technology, with another nail to hammer shut the coffin in which privacy is awaiting burial.

In the year 2002, to keep what privacy we have we must rely on our wits, but then, perhaps that is not entirely a bad thing.

Ye Gods!

THAT I DEPARTED THE RANKS OF THE CHRISTIANS I shall never regret because theirs is, on the whole, a cruel creed that has brought as much misery as joy into the world. I do regret my manner of leaving.

I was a grown man, seven or eight years gone from the family nest, and was visiting my mother and father at their farmhouse in Merlin, Ontario. When they went to St. Thomas's little brick church beside the Thames River I went with them, that summer day, just as I would have gone had they been attending a heavy horse show, a funeral or some other social occasion of the country. I went through all the standing, sitting, kneeling motions at the right times and could hear Mother, as always, saying during catechism, "From battle, murder... good Lord deliver us." She would never speak the words "and sudden death" because it wouldn't have been honest. She believed sudden death was good. Her God, with typical perversity, was to deny her that wish. The priest, a war veteran, seemed a typically likeable man, and I sat through his sermon comfortably enough, letting my mind loose to wander in the fields of imagination, probably about fornication. However, when it came time to take Communion (a ceremony in which Mother always resisted the official belief that it was a ritual act of cannibalism), I motioned my parents to go past me. Mother was aghast. She commanded me in whispers and looks to go up and take the wafer and the wine, and when I refused she and Father sat grimly with me in their seats.

I shouldn't have done that, embarrassing her in front of her friends. One more sip of sweet wine and another tasteless biscuit on my tongue wouldn't have mattered one way or another in my life. Had I been a daughter and sensitive, I would probably have taken Communion. But I was a son, thoughtless and insensitive; I didn't realize Mother wasn't fully aware that I had had my fill of virgin births and resurrections from the dead, the last named being an event that even the Apostles themselves couldn't agree on as to time and place. To me it was all bullshit.

But I could have handled it far better, taken Communion and later that day said, "Mother, there is something I have to tell you. That was my last. I have no more belief than the barn cat in the teachings of the Church. I haven't had since before I was confirmed twenty years ago."

She and Dad would never again go to church when I was with them, although they went faithfully all the many Sundays of the many years that followed when I was not visiting and they are buried in the churchyard there together now.

Unthinking and insensitive though I was, I recall that day as one more example of how organized religion creates large and small miseries in our world, large in Ulster and the Middle East, tiny, small but smarting, within my own family. Religion sometimes brings out the best in mankind but surely it also brings out the worst.

I was not completely hostile to the creed in those years. There were, as there are today, a lot of very good people who believed as well as a few very bad ones, and who could quarrel with the ascendancy of the religion's gentler aspects in most parts of the world—turn the other cheek, love thy neighbour as thyself and those wonderful words of St. Paul, "Though I speak with the tongues of men and of angels, and have not charity, I am become as sounding brass, or a tinkling cymbal." Rather than hostile, I was indifferent. Organized religion just didn't seem important enough for either time or thought. I lived with two wives during that half century, one for twenty-two years and another for seventeen years, and to this day I could not tell you the religion of either one. It never seemed worth asking about and they never asked me mine.

In this respect I anticipated the views of the majority of Canadians. By the century's end, about one in five was a declared atheist. Churches were closing down on every hand. The Roman Catholics were running out of both priests and nuns.

The fundamentalist Christians would frequently lay claim to extensive growth in their numbers but on examination these numbers tended to show that one fundamentalist group had taken parishioners from another. The total remained just about fixed.

In the rest of the world the situations varied, but the trends were the same. Americans, traditionally more fascinated with our royal family than were Canadians, also clung more to formal Christianity, not only choosing church weddings, baptism, christening and so forth but also going to church on Sundays.

The Russians also kept to the old ways longer. When released from three generations of religious suppression with the collapse of communism, their majority Orthodox Church had forgotten nothing and learned nothing. One of the first actions of this recently liberated church was to petition government to suppress other Christian denominations.

Toward the end of the twentieth century there was a worldwide development called New Religious Movements. The NRMs, focus of many studies, usually have brilliant blooms and early deaths. Some seem bizarre to most people. One, which survives after half a century, is the Cargo Cult of some South Pacific Islands, where the followers believe that by building airstrips they can entice back the cargo planes the Americans sent there during the Second World War, stuffed with pop, cigarettes, tinned Spam and all the other goodies they learned to love. Other believers, like those of the Jones cult, ended up committing mass suicides, parents feeding deadly poison to their children before swallowing it themselves with the same total faith they swallowed the original teachings. Governments, most recently the French, moved to suppress some movements, such as Scientology and the Moonies, alleging racketeering. Most fundamentalist groups, however, exude the fine elixir of faith, hope and charity and seem as blameless as well as lovable as our children. Perhaps more so than the kids.

To me this reflects the fact that people everywhere realize there is a mystery out there that science has been unable to solve for us. We keep looking, as the seed in the ground unfolds and stretches its filaments upward toward the unseen light above. Seeds, however, don't go into a lot of damn foolery about it; if they did we'd never have grown enough wheat to make a single loaf of bread. Do I sound irritable? I am.

If irritation could be raised among non-Christians, fundamentalists were the ones to do it. We all became familiar with well-dressed, polite and otherwise doubtless decent men and women who came to the door and presumed to ask us to reveal our private beliefs to them. They said God told them to. Why God didn't ask us Himself they never said.

The Roman Catholics insisted that theirs was the one true creed because it came down in direct line of apostolic succession. This meant that popes, including the liars and the fornicators, could not be wrong. Fundamentalists and many milder Protestants said much the same about the Bible. If it was in the Bible, it was true. Contradictory, maybe, but true, Gospel truth. Neither school of thought could offer an ounce of proof but this never deterred the true believers because they had their ad hominem arguments. If a deed and thought are good, then they are Christian. If all good deeds and thoughts are Christian, that proves that Christianity is good. If Christians do bad things, such as following the biblical injunction to commit genocide from time to time or kill their kids, they are not true Christians, further proving the sublimity of the Christian religion.

Few of us bothered arguing such matters although a few had the wit to try. Somebody I do not know, an anonymous person who incites in me the deadly sin of envy because of writing so much better than I do, put this on the Internet soon after a TV talk show host named Dr. Laura denounced homosexuals because the Bible said they were an abomination. She may be a relative of that popular girl, Laura Norder. I repeat the Internet comment in full:

> Dear Dr. Laura,
>
> Thank you for doing so much to educate people regarding God's law. I have learned a great deal from your show and I try to share that knowledge with as many people as I can. When somebody tries to defend homosexuals, for example, I simply remind him that Lev. 20:13 clearly states it to be an abomination. End of debate.
>
> However, I need some advice from you regarding some other laws and how I should apply them.
>
> 1. When I burn a bull on the altar as a sacrifice, I know it creates a pleasing odour for the Lord (Lev. 1:9). My problem is my neighbours. They claim the odour is not pleasing to them. Should I smite them?
>
> 2. I would like to sell my daughter into slavery, as sanctioned in Exod. 21:7. In this day and age, what do you think is a fair price to charge for a twelve-year-old whose teeth have been straightened?
>
> 3. I know I am allowed no contact with a woman while she is in her menstrual uncleanliness (Lev. 15:19–24). But how do I tell? I have tried asking and find most women take offence.
>
> 4. Lev. 25:44 states I may possess slaves, both male and female, provided they are purchased

from neighbouring nations. A friend claims that this applies to Mexicans but not to Canadians. Why can't I have a Canadian slave?

5. I have a neighbour who insists on working on the Sabbath, contrary to Exod. 35:2, so I know he must be put to death. Is it up to me or should all the neighbours take part in killing him?

6. A friend thinks that even though eating raw shellfish is an abomination (Lev. 11:10) it is a lesser abomination than homosexuality. I'm not so sure. Can you settle this point?

7. Lev. 21:20 says that I may not approach the altar of God if my sight is impaired. My sight's not so shabby, but I do need glasses for the phone book. Is there any wiggle room in this rule?

8. Almost all my male friends get their hair trimmed, including hair around their temples, even though this is expressly forbidden in Lev. 19:27. How should my friends be slain?

9. I know from Lev. 11:6 that touching the skin of a pig makes me unclean. May I still play football if I wear gloves?

10. My uncle, a farmer, violates Lev. 19:19 by planting two different crops in the same field (corn and tomatoes), as does his wife by wearing garments made of two different kinds of thread (cotton and polyester). My uncle also tends to blaspheme a lot, usually about his crops. Is it really necessary for us to turn out the entire township to stone them to

death (Lev. 24:16)? Couldn't we just burn them to death in a private family gathering, the same as we now do with people who sleep with their in-laws (Lev. 20:14)?

Thank you, Dr. Laura, for what you have done so far to remind us that God's word is eternal and unchanging.

your devoted fan
Eric

Of the Canadians who told Statistics Canada they were Christian, church attendance and other evidence indicates that they thought of their religion as something to be invoked at funerals, at weddings (for those who continued getting married in a church or married at all) and, among the old and good families, at christenings. They went along with it in the way I went along with my old parents. The fables became part of the structure of our thinking and talking, if not our belief. The same thing may be observed in Mexico, where Pentecostals may take their children to some ceremonies in the Catholic church because the ritual is so much more colourful.

The provenance of many of the fables has become clearer with recent studies. A God bedding a virgin is common enough in the Middle Eastern world. The Greeks had such legends. They are handy, I suppose, for unwed girls who found themselves introducing a tiny stranger to their very proper, if rather unworldly, families. One of the Pharaohs' daughters accomplished it by claiming she found the kid floating in the tule patch. As for rising from the dead, that repeated the story of the Egyptian god Osiris, among others. Rising from the dead or, in the case of Indian gods, being recycled by rebirth comes naturally enough to humans. We are believed to be the only species who lives with an awareness of our inevitable death. We have never liked it.

Who was Jesus? Probably more than one person, because in parts of the New Testament he speaks of love and gentleness but in others he talks like the traditional Hebrew revolutionary. "I come not to send peace, but a sword. For I am come to set a man at variance against his father, and the daughter against her mother, and the daughter in law against her mother in law" (Matt. 10:34–35).

For the true believer, nothing is too far-fetched nor, probably, can it ever be. Those of strong religious inclination will always seek to set belief above rationality and be rather proud of the accomplishment. How else can Christians claim that they worship one true God when, as an article of faith, they recognize three, God the Father, God the Son and God the Holy Ghost? The Holy Ghost God is the father of the son but the son doesn't ever say so and talks only about God the Father as father, a god who, for reasons he doesn't seem to understand, forsakes him when he is crucified.

Gospel truths such as these do not matter to most Christians. If you have the gift of faith, as many Christians as well as many Communists of my acquaintance could claim to, facts such as these do not matter. The believers cling to their redemptionist creed despite any and all evidence to the contrary.

I occasionally envied both groups their serene confidence that they had unlocked the universe's secrets and that all the treasures would be theirs in the sweet by and by, either in the Kingdom of God or in the classless, stateless society where nobody asked for your credit card.

Some may feel that I have an animus toward the Christian sect. What about the others? What of the Jews, who threw Arabs off land that they had occupied for centuries because God told them to, their other authority being the British government, which said, "Quite all right, chaps, help yourself to it, toodlepip." What of Sikhs in British Columbia, where violent quarrels erupted over such matters as whether to eat off tables in the temple? What of the Muslims who, if I spoke of their prophet as I speak of Jesus

Christ, might well publicly demand that I be murdered? The truth is, I can't afford bodyguards to protect me from Muslim fanatics, and any criticism of the Sikh community in Canada invites probes by our rulers that I lack the legal resources to combat.

Our Thought Police tolerate criticisms of Christians and Anglo-Saxons, a situation attributable to the Supreme Court Goodspeak edict that some Canadians are more equal than others. So without incurring ferocious legal expenses, I temper my criticism of religions other than the Christian. The wise reader, in whose existence I have faith, will realize that I know of no saving graces in any organized religion, although Taoism and Buddhism do seem a bit less bloody-minded than others. It's the determination to prove the unprovable, to oblige men to accept absurdity as truth, that drives the priestly clans. Of course some, including many Christian fundamentalists, claim to have no priests and invent other names for them. If any man seeks to direct your behaviour because, he says, he knows more about God than you do, that man is a priest by any definition of that word and he is a member of a hierarchy, committed to stifling inconvenient arguments, if necessary with the torture rack and the stake. Mark Twain, who had about as much religion as I do and I think compared his understanding of a church service with that of a hog in a peach orchard, frequently railed against the wilder absurdities of his day. Faith, he said, gives us comfort but doubt educates us.

By the time of Darwin, who was not the first proponent of the theory of evolution but for some reason the first to gain wide public notice when he wrote about it, there were already enough rationally minded folk on earth to doubt the bishop who claimed that the universe was 3,347 years old. Fossils and dinosaur bones had accomplished much in the healthy realms of doubt. But the great breakthrough, whereby the control of the world's largest Christian church over the masses of the people was finally shattered, was a little thing called the pill. It was anathema to popes and prelates because it promised to cancel their sect's hope of victory by the act of reproduction. Roman Catholics were no longer likely to conquer by cradle.

Almost immediately in the United States and not long after in such strongly traditional religious nations as Spain, Italy, Ireland and Quebec, the birth rate dropped with a suddenness that most people hadn't seen since the stock market experienced a readjustment in October 1929. The province of Quebec went from having the highest birth rate in the United States and Canada to the lowest in the entire western world. Quebecois saw a stark end to their society, and their frantic efforts to save it with repressive language laws and separatist movements were a predictable and natural result.

During all this the teachings of the Roman Catholic Church had not altered a hair's breadth. Birth control was a sin. This made the true nature of the change inescapably obvious. The change in the birth rate by use of the pill was a choice that could be made only by women, therefore women no longer held fully to the faith. When they rejected faith on a matter so fundamental, their menfolk rapidly followed. Again to cite the example of Quebec, long called priest-ridden Quebec, by the time I was elected to Ottawa in 1968 the Quebec members of all parties seemed to fear condemnation by labour unions, women's groups, professional groups, Native Indians or the local Chowder and Marching Society more than they feared the disapproval of their Church. The power, with the glory, had evaporated overnight.

The result of all this? Without the stability provided by Christianity, I fear for my country. This may seem contradictory but it is not illogical. The Christian religion made our society stable. Religion is not the only force for stability in society. Most Chinese, the largest aggregation of humans on earth, have lived most of their millennia with nothing closer to religion than Confucianism, which is more a code of conduct than a religion. But western man was either completely ruled or powerfully influenced by religion for nineteen hundred years, leading

Napoleon to remark, in a letter to his brother, that religion is the only force that prevents the poor from killing the rich.

What, in the absence of religion, will make Canadians and Americans ethical people? What authority will replace God in enforcing moral behaviour, an enforcement that even boasted punishment units called purgatory and hell? Men usually find ways to elude their nation's police and courts, but for nineteen hundred years they knew no ways to escape the judgment of Almighty God. God heard all, saw all and could see into their hearts and souls. This religious belief was a mighty force for peace, order and good government.

Add to this a complication. Now everybody in this country is legally a criminal, in the pure sense of that word, the pure sense being that you are a criminal if you commit murder, rape or 10,000 minor offences for which our rulers provide jail terms. In this construct the criminality is the act, not the consequences. We choose to escape the criminal label now by declaring that only people whom the rulers have caught and punished are criminals and all the rest who did the same thing but escaped punishment are not criminals, but hardly anybody believes that. Almost everybody thinks the commission of the wrongful act is the crime, not the legal proceedings that may or may not result. However, the claim "I'm not a criminal unless convicted" is a favourite of not only commercial criminals and their lawyers but also of the state itself, which recognizes that it has created more criminal offences than it could ever hope to police or prosecute.

In dealing with criminality in the pure sense of the word, we all know now that scarcely any of us can go more than a week or two without either consciously or, more likely, unconsciously committing acts for which we can be charged, tried before a jury of our peers and convicted to serve time in prison. Every Canadian walks through a minefield of laws and "regulations having the force of law," thousands of the latter being turned out by order-in-council with no reference to Parliament; he has little hope of going a week, let alone a month, without stepping on one or two of them. The only Canadians who don't break laws now are in hospitals on life support systems.

I bring to mind a case in which I contested in court a charge of crossing a solid line on a highway that happened to be empty except for me. There were two charges, I noted, which read almost identically. I asked Crown Counsel. "That's so if we miss one time we can hit you with the second barrel," he said. I liked that answer, it was so honest, for a change, but it did not build my faith in our justice system and few things have since. So, in reality, we should face the cold fact that criminal conduct is now the norm and that our hope of escaping punishment, which is considerable, is the faith that the rulers are too busy to bother applying the law to us in most cases.

But what of the general well-being of our society? Law never did serve us as well as belief in a God who knew our every thought and impulse. Without a belief in the judgment of the wisdom and power of God, what will guide us?

Some say it can be done, as does Robert Buckman in his book *Can We Be Good Without God*. Maybe. The jury is still out.

For two other reasons, the decline of religion is alarming and dismaying.

For one thing, so much of what the Christians preach is not only good but essential to our living together on the face of the earth. Hope, charity, honesty and, above all, love of one's fellow man are the very root and branch of the good life. I would also regret the loss of the magnificent English of the King James Version of the Bible but it's too late for that, the Christians themselves have already robbed the book of much of its force and beauty with the dumbing down done by the most recent translators, forcing those of us who love English to find and keep copies printed before 1982.

And, second, there is one fireproof, bombproof reason to lament the fading of religion. Whatever their failings, these are the people who have always asked the important questions. What is life about? Why are we here? What is the purpose? Whose purpose? I deal with that vast subject in another chapter. Inadequately, of course, but then, I am an inadequate man. The Christian religion got that right about us also.

Circles, Cubes and Luscious Rot

When an Englishman says the goose hangs high, he does not mean he's put it up where the cats can't get at it. He means it's rotten and therefore ready to eat. Geese, ducks and other game birds are often hung by the neck until the processes of decay have gone so far that the body falls to the floor. This is just one of the folkways of the people of the Sceptred Isle, others being a stiff upper lip, cricket and an expensive private education system called public schools that turns out graduates who haven't a single practical ability with which to earn a living. I criticize none of these folkways, it being none of my business, but offer the stinking-bird meal as an extreme example of what goes on, usually less dramatically, all over the world. Man has a taste for rot.

Alcohol and cheese are two of the well-known forms of decay that most people enjoy. There is a reason—good or bad doesn't matter, it's a reason—for delighting in alcohol. The fermentation bugs create a product that alters a human's state of mind and provides many of us with the cheery illusion that we are witty, charming and an asset to any social gathering. Cheeses, however, don't even offer the illusion of wit and charm, they simply stink. Some stink worse than spoiled game birds. Limburger, an excellent cheese from the Wisconsin Dells of America, has a smell that compounds fecal matter, rotten meat and the grunge that accumulates between the toes if you don't wash your feet often enough. It's a very tasty cheese. Some can't get past the smell to taste it, but that odour of decay is part of the taste. Smell itself is a part of our taste apparatus and people who lose their sense of smell usually can't taste any food.

A taste for what has gone bad is, it seems, universal. Almost everybody enjoys eating cheese, some choosing mild and some strong decompositions. For reasons not entirely clear, although completely nonsensical, the eating of cheese has long been associated with social rank. It's the aristocrats and their imitators who delight in Roquefort, Brie, Stilton and, from China, a similar cheeselike product called Thousand Year Old Eggs. The yeomanry of the land usually abhor such stuff and decline any cheese stronger than Cheez Whiz from a jar. However, even processed cheeses are the same stuff, milk gone buggy. And few of the villein class will reject the spoiled cabbage called sauerkraut, not to mention alcohol.

Does decay produce dietetic elements necessary for human health? There is no evidence that kids who don't get yogourt grow up mentally or physically stunted. Is it a throwback to our ancestors who were poor, weak and fearful little creatures who had to join the vultures in eating spoiled meat that the higher echelons of animals could no longer choke down? Possibly. But we lost our tails hundreds of generations ago. Surely in that length of time we could have abandoned some bad eating habits, if, in fact, they are bad.

Perhaps rotten food is good for you. Some sociologists say that rotten movies are good for us because we watch depraved behaviour instead of practising it. By extension, they might perceive that the rule applies in some way to our enjoyment of oolichan grease or Danish Blue, not to mention so elementary and simple an example as bread, in which the bubbles are produced by bacteria related to those that make alcohol for us.

I raise the matter not to offer answers—I have none—but to speculate that our strange tastes may be a tiny, visible outward sign of something important to the human soul, the soul being the only thing of any true importance. If nothing less, the discussion serves as a reminder of how little we know. Man is a small child who wonders if the trees waving is what makes the wind blow.

A few more examples of mystery? Why not?

Mathematics, the most objective of all the sciences, can teach us efficiency in a trice. The boundary of a circle contains maximum area for the minimum perimeter. So, also, when using straight lines, the square is best and the cube contains space more efficiently, as well as being more resistant to blows than the hexagon.

Apparently, we don't like this. Artists and architects have always known that human instinct is to shun the square, the circle, the cube, the sphere. We are at ease with ovals and spheroids. Many a man, particularly in pioneer days, erected a square house to save money and materials and then spent the rest of his life taking away the squareness by tacking on lean-tos, adding porches, installing dormers, offsetting doors and windows from dead centres—anything to escape the curse of efficiency. Many knew why they chose the square shape in the first place but few knew why they had a compulsion to change it later.

As for art, it also observes the rule that nature abhors a straight line. A century ago it was an article of faith that light travelled in a straight line, but Albert Einstein's theories and subsequent physical observations showed us that gravity bends it. The circle also is avoided by artists. West Coast Native art is an example. In all its multitude of shapes and endless permutations, there are no circles except for eyes on Haida totem poles, and the Haida always made a point of not being like other people.

Why should circles, cubes and squares make us uneasy? For the same reason that women offer to explain their attacks of premenstrual tension. "If you must know, it's because, that's why."

Equally mysterious, how do we learn to hate and to love the inanimate, and why?

For everybody who enjoys music of any type, there are particularly thrilling passages. One for me, in Verdi's *Il Trovatore*, is Azucena, the gypsy woman, who rises from her bed of rags and sings to her son, "Home to our mountains / Let us return, love / There in the young days / Peace had its reign. / There will thy soft song / Fall on my slumbers / There will thy lute / Make me happy again." I would like to be listening to this when I die.

Sometimes, playing it on a CD in the car, I will push the repeat button and listen to it a second time. Probably at one time or another I pushed repeat a third time. I surely never did more, because with repetition comes an inexplicable change. The music is identical. It is imbedded in plastic. It cannot alter. But the aria becomes less attractive. I leave it, it does not leave me.

If I had to hear that aria twenty times in a row, I would begin to dislike it, fifty times, I would detest it, listening to it twenty-four hours a day might drive me mad. What in these circumstances would turn my love into hatred? Boredom is no answer. Boredom and mental anguish are symptoms, not causes. Something happened to make me reject pleasure.

Do I fear that other people will think me stupid or silly to play the same melody again and again? I'm in the car, remember, with nothing but road noise around me. Add to that the fact that I don't much give a damn about other people's opinions of me. When another person has thought ill of me, I almost never set out to change that opinion and am more likely to seek ways to reinforce it. Nobody likes having to change an opinion, and if my neighbour's opinion of me be negative, let him keep it unchanged, to his comfort. The only explanation for the aria ailment that occurs to me is that a mechanism within instructs me that if I listen to and enjoy only one song, admire only one painting, love only one story, my life is, in a sense, ended. I have lost my curiosity and it is time for me to move over and make room for more open minds and open hearts.

There are other mysterious pleasures in life that add to our puzzlement. They are a major contribution to the sum of human happiness. They are balm to the soul. They are harmonious.

Try this for an example: 1.6180339887....

A meaningless figure? Far, far from it. You encounter this figure every day you live and always with a subliminal sense of pleasure. Old, tried, tested and true, 1.6180 et cetera expresses in mathematic formula the way pussy willow buds are staggered as they appear on the stalk, the breeding of rabbits, the curl of a snail's shell and the spiral nebula of which our sun system is a part. It has many names; among the better known are Golden Mean, Divine Proportion and Fibonacci numbers, the last named for an Italian mathematician who lived a thousand years ago and who first put into figures the proportion that Greek architects arrived at instinctively in building structures such as the Parthenon. Interestingly enough, this definer of one of the world's great mysteries was known to his neighbours as Blockhead; his surname itself means "Son of the Simpleton."

Where did this gift to our sense of grace come from? It doesn't fit counting by dozens, the decimal system, the binary system or the 28-day phases of the moon. It is as though it were visited upon us from a different universe or a different dimension of the universe we are in. We only know it makes us feel good.

What purpose, then, is served by these reflections, which take up so much space in this book? How can it matter that we have an inborn preference for the off-centre, the asymmetrical and the rotten? Can it matter at all? We got along fairly well for a few millennia without examining these quirks. Also, since we don't know how they lodged in our heads, how could we eliminate them even if we wished to?

We probably know more than our cousins among the apes and monkeys and our friends among the dogs but it is a knowledge very, very scant.

Since there is so much beyond our understanding, we might dismiss all such matters as being unsolvable and therefore un-important. We won't, because we are possessed of the Divine Discontent of Man, thank God, if he be there. I introduce a handful of mysteries here for one reason only, as proof that we forget all too often, and at our peril, how very little we know. Logic, reason and facts simply are not good enough. In many respects man is not a logical creature, nor ever can be. He will not live in the iron cage of rationality into which the ideologues are forever attempting to force him, with such lamentable results.

Art Outlives Us

STORYTELLING, DANCING, SONG, SCULPTURE AND PAINTING are all essential parts of human existence, as I learned late. For too much of my life I thought of them as merely frosting on life's cake. Here, I confine my comments to the only art in which I can claim any expertise, the telling of stories. Even that I once disdained and until quite late in life, after a few successes such as "The Education of Phylistine" and "Breaking Smith's Quarter Horse," stories that remained in print and copyright longer than almost any other Canadian works in the last half of the twentieth century, I was still unsure as to whether they were worth anything and nagged by the suspicion that writing was no way for a grown man to earn a living.

Now I know otherwise. Those two stories and perhaps a few others will outlive me by a generation or more. Information about whether my mortgage was paid off, the size of my credit card bills and such stuff is less than a soup made from the shadow of the wing of a passing dove. The arts live longer than anything else. Of them all, the telling of stories is one of the greatest, and those who do not do this for their grandchildren neglect both a joy and a duty. Every generation needs stories told by those who went before.

I offer an example, a classic great story. I wish I had told it but the author was an unknown Lakota who died a century or so ago. Out of a commonplace observation that men and dogs have a special relationship, he created a story that lives on as a masterpiece. This is the translation:

> In the beginning, men and the other animals were the same and could speak with one another. But the Great Spirit became angry with man and decided to separate them. He called them all

together on the floor of the desert, the man on one side, all the other animals on the other side, and with his thumbnail he made a mark in the sand between them.

The mark he made grew deeper. It went right down to the centre of the earth. It grew wider and wider, man standing on one side, all the other animals on the other side.

Just when it seemed that man was going to be alone forever the dog made a tremendous jump and took his place beside the man.

This is no old man prattling, this is an inspired professional teller of stories. All he has to offer is a commonplace, that men and dogs are close. There is nothing more, and everybody already knows it. He could have told it all in two sentences: "The Great Spirit decided to separate man from the other animals but the dog stayed with man." Exactly true but a narrative, not a story.

The difference is fundamental. Narratives are valuable, we use them all the time: they are an account, true or fictional, of a series of events. It is the twist of the narrative that creates a story that excites our imagination, touches our heart and is remembered and retold during the long dark nights of winter.

Some say there are only half a dozen stories in the world, being told again and again in endless permutations and combinations, as men create symphonies using only twelve musical notes.

Observe this Lakota professional plying his trade. First, he obtains what every storyteller needs, the willing suspension of disbelief. Did you stop reading because some being cut the planet in half with his thumbnail? The original author could have made the whole matter too easy and uneventful. The dog could have simply stepped across the line with no risk when it was only a centimetre wide. Instead he made the dog wait until the gap was almost unbridgeable. But there is a factor more important than all the preceding. It is the essence of the art of storytelling. He made his audience take part in creating the story. Any great storyteller arouses questions he does not attempt to answer. All who hear this story are left to write most of it themselves. In this story: Did the dog jump because he couldn't allow man to be alone? Did he jump because of early conditioning? Did he not know why he jumped and asked himself, once on the other side, "Why am I here?" Did the Great Spirit know all along that this would happen or was he, also, surprised? And if, to your mind, there is a clear answer to be chosen from these or other suggestions, will it still be your choice when you are older and have crossed many more hills and valleys? That is the storyteller's great art, to recognize and make use of the fact that all great stories are told one-to-one, not one to multitudes, and that each party, the teller and the listener, has a part to play in its formation.

Perhaps—I can't tell—herein is the reason that art has a longer life than we have. It is because we take part in it. Everybody has at least one good story to tell but almost all do not write it and of the few who attempt to write it, many abandon the project because of difficulties that are, in truth, more fancied than real. Yet all who read or share a story take part in the formation of that story and are, therefore, themselves artists. Without doubt a similar process exists with dancing, singing, painting, sculpture and all the rest. It is an irresistible force in our natures.

WHO IS THAT MYSTERIOUS MASKED STRANGER? IT'S YOU

IN THE DAYS WHEN PEOPLE used to offer reasons for getting divorced, a favourite in Hollywood was for one partner to say that the other didn't understand him, her or it. Why, dear Hollywood Unsophisticates, did you expect understanding? Why weren't you looking for good cooking or fun in bed, which are often attainable?

I have had two wives and I never understood either of them. I never much tried to. I tried to be a faithful, loyal friend and I never asked them to do anything they would have considered unnatural, such as plucking and cleaning ducks for me. That struck me as pretty husbandly and should have made a search for understanding unnecessary. We were different people and, although we could interbreed and sometimes did so, in many ways we seemed close to being of different species. I produced no eggs, never bled except when injured and never experienced being treated as an inferior by males, the last being a situation quite common to women in earlier decades. The reverse applies, of course. I never expected my wives or my girlfriends to spend time trying to understand me.

This worship of the word *understanding* is a recent fad. For most of the centuries we considered it something akin to purity, justice or the Peace of God, something you occasionally talked about as if it were real but never expected to see in anything approaching perfect form. Love was different. It also was a quality that could not be seen or weighed, but it could be real. Yet to understand and think and act with the heart and mind of another person was an idea all too easily adopted as a substitute for more practical activity, and now everybody is obliged to at least pretend to understand everybody else or, if not everybody else, then surely those called nearest and dearest.

There are questions about this that nobody asks. Why is it necessary for a wife to understand why her husband gets his jollies by watching some middle-aged gentlemen, hired at immense expense, try to hit a ball with a stick? Why does he need to know why, when shopping, she will buy just about any damn thing if she believes the merchant is losing money on the deal? The answer: it is not necessary. Just say "That's her nature" and go on with practical matters like taking out the garbage and keeping off the good furniture and out of bankruptcy.

Nobody talks more about the necessity of pure and perfect understanding than the chattering class, and it is the same chattering class people who spend most money lying on the psychiatrist's couch trying... Do you need to guess? No, you know. They are asking the shrink to help them understand themselves.

They fail, of course, because nobody understands himself any more than he understands other people. Every man is at least three men: the man the world thinks he is, the man he knows himself to be and the man he really is. The third is never discovered by anybody, but customers keep paying the head-shrinkers high fees trying to find out. This is one reason that a smell of humbug is always detectable on that supple, bending, flowery branch of medicine called psychiatry, the trade in which the mental disease of last year, which you poured out your treasure to have diagnosed and treated, turns out next year to have never existed. The witch doctors set out to accomplish the impossible and when they can't, they invent new illnesses they are also unable to cure.

At the close of the Second World War the American Psychiatric Association manual, called the *DSM* (for *Diagnostic and Statistical Manual of Mental Disorders*), recognized twenty-six mental illnesses. It was followed by *DSM-II*, *DSM-III* and, in 1994, by *DSM-IV*. The *DSM-IV* was 886 pages in length and the number of mental disorders ran into many hundreds. Included were such ailments as passage of feces in places not appropriate, coffee drinking and the habit of rubbing up against other people for sexual satisfaction in crowded buses. These and hundreds of other behaviours are indications that it is time to cast yourself on the couch and try to sort out your brain.

Equally interesting are the old mental diseases that have disappeared. The diagnosis of dementia praecox, so popular in past decades, turns out to have been in error. There is no such mental illness. Sorry about that. Autistic children, it turns out, have a physical malfunction of the brain; they were not made that way by cold, distant, unloving mothers. Families that were ruined by the earlier diagnosis of heartlessness may take what comfort they can from the fact that it was all some psychiatrist's imagination. We may expect the same, a few years hence, with the casting off of the recovered memory mental condition, in which angry young women, coached by psychiatrists, have been able to send bewildered and heartbroken fathers to jail for imagined sexual molestation. These fads are not merely expensive, they sometimes cause irreparable tragedies. There has, of course, never been a case of a psychiatrist compensating or even apologizing to people whose money he took to treat imaginary maladies, any more than we may expect the Roman Catholic Church to regret that it had created so many imaginary saints to whom the people prayed for help in centuries past.

Let's be fair, although it's a practice I had thought to put behind me in this book. Often the people did obtain mental and spiritual help from those saints who never existed, and many people today are helped by psychiatric diagnoses that may be just as spurious as the saints. More can be accomplished by faith than most men imagine. Neither are people possessed of an unreasonable quota of faith in this and that deterred by revelations that the words were written on fast, running water. Those who trust the psychiatrists' latest popular mental malady will easily overlook the fact that this was the profession that once recognized a mental disorder called drapetomania, described as the desire of a slave to escape from slavery. There will always be some customers for the saints, the shrinks and the Brooklyn Bridge salesman (see chapter called "How to Tell Sheepshit from Boston Baked Beans").

So people should not expect that the next catalogue, *DSM-V*, will be less than 1,000 pages long. Bipolar may go the way of dementia praecox but scores of new manias will have been identified. Failure breeds enthusiasm. Consider law. When we find that the creation of a multitude of laws only increases the number of criminals, we react by passing yet more laws in the sublime faith that just a few more will do the trick. So it is with psychiatry, which entered its popular period under the leadership of Sigmund Freud, an Austrian scientist who faked his studies and, having stood much of the world on its head, is now generally discredited at century's end on account of lying so much.

Ordinary people, however, almost every one of whom is not crazy, no matter what statistics you may see, would do well to do as they have always done: trust common sense more than experts. Common sense suggests we abate some of today's passion for the mystic quality called understanding. It exists, but in very small quantities. Your mother probably came as close as anyone can to understanding you and likely as not even she gave up on you once you reached your teens.

Opponents of this thought may well say, "If we make no effort to understand or to be understood, how can we live? What hope can there be for humankind to live together?"

There are several answers to that. One is rather facile but it is worth mention: we have all too much togetherness already. Individuals should be trying to find ways to put more space around ourselves. The people who study demographics tell us that there seems to be an end in sight to the overbreeding by humans and that by the mid-twenty-first century the world's population should begin to decline. However, they say by then there will be fifteen billion of us, which is ten or twelve billion too many for comfort.

As somebody with my tastes once wrote: "Good clean air from east to west / And room to go and come / I love my fellow man the best / When he is scattered some."

Forgetting the billions and returning to tiny, personal matters, which are more comprehensible, I observe that my father got along all right without being understood. The notion simply did not interest the man. He could be charming, and usually was. Animals and little children loved him, perhaps because he let them get a little closer to his soul than adults, who might mess it up. In the sum of his life, my father harmed no man, he left the world a little better place than he found it, he was respected and he died reasonably happy except for the illusion on his last night that somebody was serving him a fish dinner, a dish he despised. I have very little idea who the man was, even less than he had. When we both knew he was dying he said only, "Well, I guess there's nothing I need to tell you about." He could have told me where his will was but it turned out there wasn't a will. Since I was then the only heir, he saw no need for one and saved a $15 legal fee. My father was a keen student of the dollar. But I won't analyze him here. I am reasonably sure he would not want me to know or go prying into the matter of his private character. Does it matter? He valued his privacy and in a sense it is good that he died before the new style of Canadian government was here to snatch the last shreds of it away from him.

However, the distant prospect of a decline in the world population is not much of a solution to the problem of how we are to get along together if I am correct in the view that understanding one another is never going to amount to much in practical terms. There are other things, more sensible, for us to do.

One means of our rubbing along somehow without too much friction is an old and excellent method, which will work within our families, in our community and in our nation. It is called courtesy.

I don't claim to be an expert. I was a slow learner. But I knew the value of it once I wrapped my stiff, stubborn mind around the idea that you catch more flies with honey than you do with vinegar. (Why is it that I admire old wives' sayings such as this one and snort when I hear the Shared Psychotic Disorder used to describe somebody who catches the Little Green Martian story from another nut? It's because that's my nature, that's why.)

A degree of courtesy comes naturally to humans as well as to quite a few of the other animals but, better news yet, courtesy can be developed and strengthened throughout a lifetime. There is a method for developing extended courtesy, rules that can be taught, memorized and practised daily. They are called good manners. Like most people, I have seen a few marriages break up. There wasn't one that might not have been saved with good manners.

This was a traditional strength of the English aristocrats. They were married off, quite often, for dynastic reasons rather than affection and like husbands and wives all over the world they eventually became a bit bored with one another. They remained wedded, continued civilized and dwelt in more or less pleasant circumstances by the constant use of good manners. Manners are, after all, nothing more than a recognition that you can avoid hurting the feelings of those you meet by the words you speak and the grace you exhibit. Thus the mark of a true gentleman or lady: to be kind and polite to people from whom they had nothing to gain and from whom they had nothing to fear. Courtesy is human warmth and let it not be said that it is nothing more than that. It is nothing less than that and our world spins better for it.

Finally, we are better off when we learn to repay discourtesy with more of our own courtesy. Remember when you want to snap at some store clerk who has treated you rudely that you have no way of knowing what troubles, what bad news, what near-intolerable suffering that man or woman may be experiencing this day. Think of that and, on your side, a little humility is seldom misplaced, being as it is a capacity to remember that we are all human and all imperfect.

How to Run the Country

Henry Ford Freed Us, the Rulers Retaliated

ORIGINALLY I LOVED OLD HENRY FORD because he built my first car, a 1926 Model T that I bought for $15. With a friend's help I pushed it out of the barn where it had been crouching for a few years and onto a country road at Cow Bay, Nova Scotia, and learned to drive it by steering down the middle of the road and only going into the ditch from time to time. Tin Lizzy was a joy. You could lean off the gas mixture with a button inside the car, reducing the gas intake until she gasped and the valves, no doubt, turned white hot. She would also run on gasoline mixed with diesel, which was even cheaper than gas, and gas was not pricey in the 1930s. Although you had to work the windshield swipes by hand, she originally had a self-starter. But when I replaced a brake band in the old planetary transmission with a new one speckled with metal, the starter permanently shorted out and thereafter I had to back off the spark, so the handle wouldn't kick my thumb off in cranking, and whirl the front crank around until she coughed to life. There was always a bit of a connection of the gears within the crankcase and as a result during cranking Lizzy would nuzzle your shoulder, like a friendly horse, and slowly back you up against the garage wall.

But that was first love and alas we all grow older. I turned my attention to sex and drinking, and cars became less important, although I have never lost my passion for them and at the time this is written own four, ranging from a thirty-year-old Datsun to a BMW. Later I returned to my love of old Henry, but for a reason much more profound than his cars, a reason sensed by Aldous Huxley in *Brave New World*. In his brave new society people used the word *Ford* as we use *God*. They said, "Ford help us," "Ford knows" and "For the love of Ford." Mr. Huxley found no better name for a supreme being, although in the world he portrayed the results of Ford's genius had been frightful. Not so in our world. Nobody at the turn of the twentieth century did more than Henry Ford to liberate the common man. Not surprisingly, he invited retaliation from our rulers, but that came later.

He was a simpleton genius, not the first nor the last to appear in this book. Jews didn't like him because he swallowed the Protocols of Zion hoax. The Brits didn't like him because he tried to stop them and the Germans from destroying a generation of their young men in the Lowlands with his loony Peace Ship experiment. But does any of that really matter? Everybody has a few crazy notions. Henry Ford's genius was not in the area of religion, politics or even mechanical engineering; his genius was social engineering. He took a process established in the 1800s, the production line method of manufacture, and combined it with a brand-new thought—he would make cars not as luxury items for the rich but as useful things for the poor. There were, after all, so many poor people out there to sell to. Three-quarters of a century later the same sort of thinking has made the personal computer a household item. At full production the Ford plant sold Model Ts for $400 each and made a handsome profit. In Canada Ford charged $500 each. When Henry was asked why, he answered, "Because the Canadians will pay it."

Why can't you and I think so clearly and become a rich philanthropist like Henry Ford? It's because almost all of us are trapped in the stinking cages of old, stale thinking into which we were born. Even when handed the key, most of us are reluctant to turn the lock and step outside.

When Henry put us on wheels he changed the whole society. Men were no longer bound to the little patch of ground where we were born. Overnight, the common man became individually mobile, with a freedom of movement formerly possessed only by the very rich, who were supposed to have deserved it, or the very, very poor, like Prairie Indians and eccentric traders and trappers, who offended public morals by having a freedom they apparently did not deserve.

Suddenly, thanks to the cheap automobile, we could move ourselves, our families, our pots and pans, our tools, our skills and our hopes and dreams anywhere the roads ran. The roads soon ran everywhere until, today, there is no piece of ground in the continental United States more than eighteen miles from a travelled road.

Americans were the first to initiate freedom of movement and Canadians followed very closely. In some parts of the world people are still catching up with the idea that every household needs at least one car in the yard but it's always an idea they welcome once it reaches them.

Ecologists, town planners, sociologists and others of that ilk, people of small imagination but boundless personal ambition, try to drag us out of our cars. They would cram us back into city tenements we fled from and give us bread and circuses to keep us quiet. They keep explaining what nobody needs explained, that a neighbourhood can be created in a city where almost all human needs can be met with stores stacked one on the other and psychodynamically designed playgrounds for the kids to use, under close supervision, during any hours that they are not attending anger management therapy. It makes sense, from their point of view. Crowds are easier to control than individuals; individuals keep haring off in their own directions for any old reason, good or bad, often as not using their cars for the purpose. Grounded, they might be quieter. The Romans managed to control their city people for hundreds of years. However, a lot of us have learned a few things since Roman times.

One of the encouraging features of today's societies is that the people keep telling the planners to take their tenements and cram them into that part of their body where the sun does not shine. Wherever and whenever it is possible, people quit public transit systems. In their own car, they may sit and grumble by the hour on gridlocked streets, thinking of the tax dollars they spend to subsidize transit riders, poisoning the sky with exhaust fumes, but in London, Rome, Paris, Oslo or Washington and New York they persist, unstructured, unproletarian, rascals to the end, the people Henry Ford knew.

The attempt to stuff people back into tenements with fruity names such as townhouses is only one backlash by the rulers against Mr. Ford. Another, a more serious one, developed early in the age of the automobile and scarcely anybody noticed, although it was the pivot on which swung the balance between the state serving man and man serving the state. Why didn't we notice? Why didn't I, for six or seven decades? We just didn't, that's all. It became accepted in nation after nation that driving a car was not a right but a privilege, granted by the state.

The difference between a freeborn right and a privilege is profound. It is the difference between being in the Don Jail and attending a Boy Scout summer camp. In both places your health and safety are well cared for, in both you have to make your own bed and brush your teeth each day, and in both food tends to be nourishing rather than tasty. The difference is that the state doesn't order Boy Scouts to go to a camp and doesn't insist that they remain there once in it.

For another easy comparison, take walking. Until very recently, everybody thought we had a right to walk anywhere on public land. Public land, we thought, was our land. We couldn't walk through police lines at a multiple murder scene and we would be discouraged from going to Mass at the cathedral buck naked, but by and large the right to propel ourselves on our own legs was almost as natural as breathing and we asked nobody's permission. This, a classic among all the freedoms, is now also under attack by the rulers and there are today sections of public parks where you may not tread unless licensed to do so. It is part of our continued descent into a police state. Twenty years ago the right of rulers to issue walking licences for public land, as they now do for

Vancouver Island's West Coast Trail, would have been as unthinkable in Canada as the issuance of licences to smell flowers.

A privilege is something granted to us by people more powerful than we are. It is, at bottom, a charitable donation from somebody in authority who has a barrel or a shipload of such privileges to pass out. Since the privilege is something only the grantor possesses, he has limitless right to choose those who will receive and those who will not. Nobody can demand a privilege with any assurance of getting anything except the back of somebody's hand.

Should the state choose that blue-eyed people shall have the privilege to drive and brown-eyed people shall not, where is there a prohibition writ? Brown-eyed and blue-eyed drivers are a long bow to draw but consider what we already have. In many jurisdictions, driving privileges are withdrawn not because the driver is unable to pass tests as to safety, not because the driver has a bad safety record, not because he is a drunk or can be shown to be in any way a threat to others but solely for the reason that he has had too many birthdays. That happened to my mother in Ontario, a woman who had an accident-free record of seventy years long. She was a fast driver, but a safe one.

Had our fathers and grandfathers been vigilant enough to make natural justice a part of the law regarding the automobile, would much have changed? Would we not still require laws relating to speed, safety, abstention from drugs and more? Of course we'd need them. Who would want to drive a car in a land where people made their own choices whether to drive on the right- or left-hand side of the highway? Much legislation would be exactly as it is today, but the spirit of our motor vehicle law and of a thousand other similar laws passed since, which glorify the state and diminish the citizen, would be different and each law would pass with more care. The country needs a Locrian Party. In the Parliament of Locria, when a legislator rose to propose a new law imposing on the freedom of citizens, as practically every law does, he wore a piece of rope around his neck that he did not remove until the legislation passed. If it did not pass, he was instantly strangled. Those were the good old days.

There is, of course, one more reason that the state's assumption of privilege in the automobile age was not resisted as it should have been. A reason it went largely unnoticed is our courts, sometimes the last pool of common sense into which we can dip to calm and clean ourselves. Judges routinely ensure, by cunning processes, that all but the most heinous of bad drivers retain the ability to move themselves around. The man forbidden to drive anywhere may yet be permitted to drive to and from his work. The bad driver ruled off the highway is provided opportunities to train himself. We might expect the same common sense judges to somehow fail to jail some old chap who wanders unshorn, unshriven, unlicensed into a public park to pick mayflowers or have a pee.

When, then, might the rulers return to the people the freedom they took, our natural right to move from place to place being one of the most fundamental but by no means the only one? Never is too long a time. All wrongs are redressed someday. Someday we will examine the rulers' assumption of the power to grant and withhold natural freedoms. How much public treasure might we have saved, how much crime might we have avoided, if in 1910 we had told the people recommending prohibition of narcotics that men and women had the natural right to fuddle their brains with drugs if they chose. Sanity eventually overtakes us all, the ruled as well as the rulers. It will not be in my lifetime or my children's; it might come in my grandchildren's when a minority movement for freedom becomes a majority movement, as happens. Meanwhile, speaking with the many while thinking with the few, I urge those children and grandchildren to move in the bureaucratic tangled jungle with the caution native to free creatures. Take the coyote for your example. The target of extermination in much of the North American continent, he has spread from the Mexican desert to the Arctic and from the western ocean to the eastern ocean. In the Vancouver area, where the species was unknown half a century ago, he lives and thrives in suburbia and even within the big city itself. He is like one of the characters in a Damon Runyon story who neither works nor wants nor goes to jail. The average car driver can surely do as well if he applies his natural instinct for caution, never drawing attention to himself, sometimes turning the system so it works for him instead of against him, seeking quiet support from his fellows; above all, privately, quietly, ridding himself of the falsehoods with which we have lived, unquestioningly, for far too long.

WHO REALLY RUNS THE COUNTRY?

MUCH OF MY LIFE HAS BEEN WASTED on shooting ducks, fixing old cars and daydreaming, but I regret none of that loss of time because it was enjoyable, and enjoyment is better than mere profit and advancement in this world. What I do regret are the hours and the anguish I wasted in combatting conspiracies. Much of my life I seemed to be facing one damn conspiracy after another, all of them powerful and most of them sinister. It was a public duty to expose them and thus weaken their grip on our society. Of course, I was not alone in this. Most of us perceive conspiracies around us, although different conspiracies suit different paranoids, and in the political world it's a rare day that passes without evidence being found of three or four grand plots against nation or yourself.

Let us count just a few historic ones. The Roman Catholic Church found a Protestant conspiracy to rule the world and the Protestants found agents of the Pope under every bed. England, in the age of the first Elizabeth, had Popish plotters spying for Spain, a few real, most imaginary, and there was a witch hunt equal to the Great Bolshevik Conspiracy that, if John Birch Society members could be believed, almost took over and ran the United States of America later. For a century after the French Revolution, Europe's monarchies battled republican conspiracies, a few of which succeeded. Josef Stalin, who apparently had a chemical imbalance of the brain, tried to find a cure by killing 25 million of his fellow citizens and never did succeed in finding all the demons he sensed were plotting against him. The Americans, perhaps because they are so wealthy that they don't have better things to do with their time, twice warped their entire society hunting the Bolsheviki, for twenty years after the First World War and for forty years after the Second.

Few nations have chosen to be so victimized by conspirators as the Americans, beginning with the poor, addled old ladies they hanged as witches at Salem and reaching a pinnacle, of sorts, with the Great Communist Conspiracy of the '50s, '60s, '70s and '80s. Tens of millions of otherwise rational Americans became frightened and angry as they peered at maps showing the red tide rising all over the globe. Stories like "Little Red Riding Hood" were yanked from school libraries and squalid people such as J. Edgar Hoover and Senator Joe McCarthy became national heroes. The Godless Reds sold drugs to the schoolchildren, encouraged riots and civil disobedience, organized labour unrest and taught children to hate their parents. Then the big scare suddenly ended in the early '90s, fading just as quickly as it had bloomed, partly because of the discovery that the Communists weren't able to feed themselves, let alone take over running the entire planet.

All of America's problems should have ceased. However, after Communism's collapse there continued to be drug sales in the schoolyards, civil disobedience, labour unrest and rebellious children, so the conspirators are apparently still at it but now we don't know who they are any longer. In 2001 a sort of substitute appeared in the Muslim al-Qaida, a modern form of the ancient Assassin Sect. These people managed to kill a few thousand in New York and Washington, many more than the few hundred slain by the Americans' own citizen fanatic Timothy McVeigh, but to those of us who lived through the Evil Empire threat (some of us twice), the public perception of the peril was never as great as that achieved by the Bolsheviki, and in 2002 very few people searched the broom closet every night before going to bed, checking for mullahs who had disguised themselves to look like ordinary burglars and rapists.

The Russians had their own conspiratorial opponent. They perceived a mighty beast of what they called fascism. Even worse, they discovered that their greatest enemy had been nourished in their own bosom, Leon Trotsky. His was the sinister mind behind those people who were almost but not quite Communist. Those almost but not quite Communists, being practically identical to the real kind, were the very foulest kind of people, worse than any other enemies, and Stalin had to have Trotsky murdered lest the Soviet state collapse. However, the Communists never seemed to have the time or the know-how for good conspiracy propaganda, and their witch hunts tended too often to be mere rant, a poor second to the tactics used by the gang led by McCarthy and Senator Robert Kennedy of the notorious Kennedy bunch.

We've always had our share of conspiracies in this country. During both world wars Canada was menaced by Germans of the second and even the third generation. The name was enough to convict them. It was in the blood. On the West Coast we rounded up all our Japanese Canadian citizens and put them in concentration camps, in part to protect them from mobs that were prepared to burn and riot in the Nisei residential and business districts but also in part because we believed that every Japanese Canadian fisherman was mapping our coast and mailing the stuff to Japan, where presumably they didn't have any maps of Canada. The absurdities go on and on. In the Korean War we discerned Chinese agents here.

Many Italians have been convinced for decades that the Masons are a more powerful and sinister group than the Mafia. As for the Muslim world, conspiracy is everywhere but there the conspirators are usually themselves, Muslims of another sect.

Because of my newspaper training to never believe a political story until it has been denied, I remained moderately sane during the Great Communist Conspiracy. That does not mean I was immune to the virus. When I was socialist or near socialist in my views, I could clearly perceive a huge right-wing conspiracy. In British Columbia it was headed by a Kelowna hardware merchant named William Andrew Cecil Bennett. He socialized more of the province with his seizures of ferries and hydro than any other premier before or since, including the avowedly socialist ones. No matter. Doing socialist things was just a ruse. The hidden agenda of conspirators often requires that they appear to adopt their opponents' policies. All we conspiracy watchers learn that.

Later, when I veered over into liberalism and conservatism, I still thought I saw other submerged, largely invisible groups that sought to run the country. I suspected a vast conspiracy of bureaucrats for a long time, despite abundant evidence that by training and nature the typical bureaucrat is mostly interested in pay, perks and pensions and seldom seeks to go to the front of the herd.

Nevertheless, my bureaucrat conspiracy theory became almost an obsession when I went to Ottawa and found how much power they held. I had been forewarned by Dimche Belovski, Yugoslav ambassador from Tito's regime. He told me, "Your country has the most powerful and most arrogant bureaucracy of any nation outside the Iron Curtain." It was, he suggested, even stronger than Yugoslavia's, although that country had dodged outside the curtain.

When you are told of a problem you will usually find it, and it did not take one long in Ottawa to learn that the old sermons about bureaucrats merely carrying out policies but never making them, being on tap but never on top, were more of the usual pious cant. Bureaucrats created most of the policies and used the elected people to bring them into effect. Only people who have spent time in capital cities know that the television show *Yes, Minister* was more fact than fiction.

What seemed a moment of truth came for me in Beijing. We were the first government delegation to China, and on the eve of our meeting with Premier Zhou Enlai we were holding talks in a large, empty hotel lobby far from microphones. Mitchell Sharp, Minister for External Affairs (as we called it in those days because we couldn't decide if the Brits were foreigners), conducted the meeting. The question of the Ming ships arose. We built the freighters in the Second World War and sent them to Chiang Kai-shek, but the Communists had seized them and were using them without paying. I recollect that the decision was to mention them but to keep the mention in perspective. Our new recognition of the Communist government was of more importance than a few rusty old freighters. Our Canadian ambassador wound up the discussion saying: "It's agreed then. All we have to do is check it back to Ottawa."

"I'm here," said Mitchell Sharp in a soft voice.

"No," said the ambassador, "I mean check back to headquarters in Ottawa." He knew where the department was run.

"I am here," the minister repeated. "There will be no call to Ottawa." The ambassador was clearly puzzled. He was not accustomed to a politician running the department. Doubtless, despite the minister's order, he checked back to the deputy minister on the telephone later that night.

It was all nourishing to a mind eager to discover our secret rulers. Yet why did I overlook some of the most obvious facts? Time after time, in public life or in private life, a major bureaucracy proves too inefficient to organize a washup in a brewery. Typically, our federal bureaucracy couldn't get an extradition order down to Mexico in time for it to be effective because nobody knew whether Mexico was in North America, Central America or South America and it kept getting into the wrong diplomatic mail bag. The bigger a bureaucracy, the less effective it is for any useful work beyond pruning radishes. Bureaucrats do not conspire to establish dictatorships; they don't think that big. Most of their days are spent in making big jobs out of little ones. Instead of sending a log through the sawmill to produce many two-by-fours, they can process a single two-by-four to create logjams.

A Mexican anecdote says more about bureaucracy than most school texts. "Is it true that bureaucrats do not work in the afternoons?" says one Mexican to another. The other answers, "No, that is not correct. Bureaucrats do not work in the mornings. In the afternoons they go home."

Who runs a department? Who runs Parliament? Who runs Canada?

I used to call these secret societies of my imagination Machiavellian, until I was rid of that error by the late Pat Terry, an old-style newspaperman ("Three times I left this business and three times I returned like a dog to his vomit"). Pat, who had the advantage of a good English liberal arts education, remarked one day: "People who compare premiers and presidents and dictators to Machiavelli really should try reading the book sometime. They should start with the book's title, *The Prince*. Machiavelli had nothing to say to kings."

Was there then no grand design by Premier Bennett to make this province conservative, no plot by communists to infiltrate other organizations with an aim to unsettling the government? Did not leading businessmen seek to create a favourable climate for their enterprises? Of course they did. There would be something very wrong with all of them if they didn't. Each group had the object of advancing its cause. The advancement of some cause is why we organize ourselves in the first place, whether it be to advance communism or build more Little League baseball fields. The weakness of the grand conspiracy idea was in the performance. None was able to bring it off.

There have been a few successes in history. Jesus Christ, starting with only ten disciples, launched a system that took over most of Europe. France's republicanism had similar successes and the Americans first conspired before they achieved their successful rebellion against Great Britain. In truth every change in society begins with very few people. A majority has never created a majority movement. But all the other forms of rule, religious, republican or rebellious, never achieved a complete success. At best they became briefly dominant. Somehow the thought of any of them taking over Canada puts too much of a burden on the imagination, even a fevered imagination. When old enough to know better I recalled a Canadian Communist of my acquaintance who was prominent enough to be denied entry into the United States, lest he overthrow that republic. He once complained to me: "People think we are taking over Canada. They have no idea how hard I work to get half a dozen members out for a discussion."

The same applies for an organization formed in the '70s known as the Trilateral Commission. It is a meeting, always private, of captains of industry, politicians and academics who, ranking high in their particular trades, could be assumed to be planning world domination. I never approached the exalted status of guest and would have been likely to attend only as one with a napkin on my forearm, pouring expensive wine at the dinner tables, so I cannot speak of it firsthand. However, knowing some of those who did, I'm sure it was no more than shop talk in some comfortable resort that served good food and had a golf course, and I have much the same certainty about the World Government people whom today's bedwetters perceive to be in control of the United Nations.

Meetings of the World Bank and the leading industrial nations of the world are much the same. There is talk, which may or may not be worthwhile, and the issuance of bland pronouncements on the need for a better, finer, purer world of prosperity and peace, one where all those spoiled, rich, pot-smoking kids outside who are fighting the policemen will turn to soccer and other healthy sports instead.

As for captains of industry running our planet, by the time a man has floated to the top of a major international corporation, pretty well all the brains and spirit have been kicked out of him and he just marks time to pension while attending conferences here and there.

Until our professional malcontents, the inheritors of the rabid Trotskyites and Stalinists, made a fuss about the World Bank meetings and other similar bunfights, very few people in the world even knew when or where the meetings were held and if they did know, they didn't much care. No doubt it is a conspiracy of sorts for those invited to attend—they conspire each time to hold another meeting on the expense account—but the hysterics of professional agitators are needless and tiresome. Increasingly these protesters are using violence instead of words and at one recent meeting an Italian policeman, fearing for his life, shot and killed one of them. My instinct was to try to get the policeman's full name from the Italian government. It's too late for sons for me, but I might yet have another grandson who could be named after him.

In the face of all the evidence that men are weak and fallible and seldom succeed in any conspiracy larger than one big train robbery, I nevertheless allowed myself to let one conspiracy hobgoblin after another ride on my shoulders for most of my life. The man who got rid of them, who crystallized my growing doubts by the application of simple common sense words, was old Mitchell Sharp, for whom I was, for a time, parliamentary secretary. He was a bureaucrat turned politician and was successful at both. A Winnipeg boy, he could still waltz on skates in his seventies, play the piano fairly well, and he married three times, the last time when he was 79 years old. He had one quality that distinguishes big men. He was decisive.

"Why is it people keep asking who really runs the country?" he said. "The answer is obvious enough. Nobody runs the country." He went on to say that Canada, like all the other countries, moves at its own speed in its own way, influenced by leaders in politics, business and the arts but never, ever, truly under their control or even their direction. All the things that happen are the result of a multitude of private decisions, privately taken for what the citizen considers to be his personal good.

For all the collectivization that has taken place, the ordinary man still thinks and acts for himself and for his family. At the invitation of others, he may, from time to time, join a noisy parade to somewhere but he never forgets where home is and he always returns to it. He is far stronger than any conspiracy and usually proves it when the occasion demands, praise be.

How We MPs Saved the Lemmings

YOU MAY HAVE NOTICED that in this book I speak with a tone of authority designed to give readers the false impression that I always know what I'm talking about. I may be wrong but I am never in doubt. Some may offer unkind criticism of this tendency of mine. However, there are important provinces in our world where there are no certainties for anybody. Humour is one. Another is politics, politics being the art of contriving ways for us to get along with one another.

Elsewhere in this book I deal with the shape of politics in those familiarly authoritative tones I refer to here, but it seems to me the subject deserves more than clinical examination of a political system. The reader should know where I come from. As an aid, this chapter is about what I did in politics, not what I thought, if, indeed, I thought much at all. I loved half of it and hated half of it and often have difficulty now remembering which half was which. As my best friend said about the war when he came home, "I wouldn't have missed it for a million dollars and I wouldn't do it again for a million."

When I accepted an invitation to be a Liberal candidate for the federal Parliament I was not a member of that party, a circumstance that did not strike me as in any way strange, but then, many of my notions about the political process were strange. In my case it was also debatable whether or not I was a philosophic liberal either but that was quite all right, because nobody then or now is precisely sure what one is. For Canadian purposes, a Liberal can be almost anybody who isn't far enough to the left or the right to be called a fanatic.

At that time, 1968, our second biggest province, Quebec, had elected practically nobody except conservatives for generations, but circumstances were such that they were required to call themselves Liberals. Others were similarly vague about exactly what a liberal philosophy was. It had something to do with Adam Smith, history's most misquoted economist. The foamy-mouthed Amurrica Firsters and Amurrica, Love It or Leave It lads associated all liberals with long hair on men and similar failings. Liberals in Canada welcomed their views because to be disliked by the flat earth people of the American Right did harm to no man.

In 1968, when I ran for nomination in the riding of Coast–Chilcotin in British Columbia, I knew one simple truth about the Liberal Party, that it was the natural governing party of Canada, a view that I and a working majority of all Canadians hold to this day.

So I went to a nomination meeting in the little logging town of Squamish, forty miles from Vancouver, and my wife and three children came dutifully as a political family should. The girls pleaded with me to not snap my braces while speaking, but I did anyway because although I appeared totally at ease, a handy quality I'd enjoyed for years, I was in fact quivering and needed all the support I could find, including braces to hold up my pants.

Jean Chrétien came to speak at my first campaign meeting, narrowly missing breaking his neck when the little plane in which he was riding made a faulty landing in Squamish harbour. He was then a very junior minister of the government and hardly worth anybody's notice, although my thoughts remained sufficiently collected in some part of my brain that night that I sensed the audience warming to this man. In the following years, when he was still almost unnoticeable on the national scene, he came to other meetings of mine and again I noticed that more than any other guest speaker, the audience wanted to come up and shake his hand later. This is because these people of the audience, very ordinary people themselves and almost all of them quite unskilled in matters political, possessed a much better ability than I did to recognize what politicians call the royal jelly. By the time that four-and-a-half-year Parliament ended, I too had recognized that this man had the jelly, so much so that years later, when he became prime minister of Canada, I was not in the least surprised and felt and said that I had seen it coming. I say all these things about Jean not to praise his works or to condemn them but to emphasize that much of politics is a realm of the strange and sometimes almost inexplicable, also to point out that public instinct is apt to be correct just as often as the preachments of the experts.

To my descendants a century or so on, if indeed there is anything recognizable as a parliamentary democracy left in your time, which I doubt, you would be well advised to scrutinize the pronouncements of political forecasters, usually called pundits, with a high-power microscope. Almost always you will find that their forecasts are that what happened last year is going to happen next year. Even more than army generals, political pundits fight the battles of the previous war.

Chrétien's mastery of a crowd was only one of several political lessons offered up to me during that campaign. Among the delegates at the nomination meeting was Margaret Murray of the *Bridge River–Lillooet News*, a lifelong Liberal Party figure except for a brief period when she ran as a Social Credit Party candidate for no apparent reason except that her husband, George, was at that time a Liberal Member of Parliament. Margaret (she hated being called Ma but accepted it for the usual political reasons) came to support another candidate, a gentlemanly fellow who was, I suspect, much more sincere about wanting to be an MP than I was.

Margaret had dismissed me in an editorial the week before as the "so-called voice of the Chilcotin" and during the later election campaign she stayed sternly aloof and never spoke for me at a political meeting or even attended one. She referred to me then as "that little turd." This was interesting later because for my entire term of office Margaret told other people publicly and me privately that my becoming an MP was all her idea, that she was the one who had led me into politics, and she could quote words of encouragement she offered to me at that time urging me on to Ottawa. I never argued the point. In politics you do not argue with people who buy their ink by the barrel. Anyway, I have no doubt that she believed it and had completely forgotten that she sat out the entire campaign. In politics you get so you can believe almost anything that seems convenient to some purpose, and I shall be most grateful if I can pursue this chapter to its conclusion without reporting some fiction that in my mind has become pure, solid, oak-ribbed, copper-bottomed fact. It is the difference between wishing something were true and it being true. One substitutes for the other, particularly for true liberals who are devoted to the perfectibility of man, while pure conservatives believe we are all born with original sin.

The third lesson of the nomination was how quickly and easily friends can be forgotten in that strange business. The man who nominated me was a Chilcotin rancher, Cecil Henry, also known as "Hungry Henry" for the time when as a hungry young cowboy he had eaten all the lunches of a six-man hay crew while delivering them by saddle horse. Cecil had little concern about politics and I wonder, now, if he had a party card either, but he spoke very effectively in that little hall in terms that people wanted to hear. "He knows every rancher in Chilcotin by his first name" was one of the lines. Untrue, of course, but a good line; it may have been the reason that in a three-way race (there was one other surprise candidate of no visible means of support) I got more than 50 percent on the first ballot.

Years later, visiting Cece Henry's area with Mitchell Sharp, who was deputy prime minister, I took Mitchell trout fishing on another rancher's territory and never so much as invited Cecil and his wife over for a coffee. The thought simply did not enter my head. It should have. It didn't. I had no thoughts for anything except catching fish. It was inexcusable but it was not uncommon, and politicians of higher rank take great care to hire executive assistants who never permit that sort of thing to occur. I always felt badly about it but what is there to say? "You weren't important enough to remember, Cecil"? It's the blind alley a politician sometimes walks into. "Why, Mrs. Gunderson, how you've changed over the years. I would never have recognized you if it weren't for your dress." We laugh with tears in our eyes.

There were a lot of new boys like me in Ottawa in 1968, swept in by Trudeaumania. We all knew where we were but we weren't entirely sure how we had gotten there. "I wanted to be a judge, that's why I ran," said Terry Murphy from the Sault. "My wife hasn't stopped crying since election night," said another MP from Toronto. I advised them all, cogently I think, that we were there because we were all exhibitionists, and if we hadn't been elected to Parliament we would probably have gone to jail for exposing ourselves to small children. "I did that," said Doug Hogarth of New Westminster, "and they elected me."

We were all in terror of making our first speech in the Green Chamber, called breaking the maiden. Now and then an MP is elected who never does it and sits silent in the House throughout a Parliament or sometimes two Parliaments, he being a good man on constituency work.

We had such a one in the BC contingent that year, Doug Stewart of Okanagan–Kootenay, a young lawyer. One of the first duties impressed upon new boys of all the parties was to be present in the House for votes, because governments rise and fall by majority votes in the Commons. Indeed, by the time the year 2000 arrived, that was about the only reason left for the existence of government MPs. When the strident bells clamoured in the big stone corridors of the Parliament Buildings we rushed to the chamber that we might rise and bow to Mr. Speaker, registering a vote to keep the government in power or to throw the rascals out depending on which party we belonged to. For the first month or two, it was the only recorded action any of us took to make Canada a better place. All except Doug, who seemed to spend twenty-three hours of each day shouting into his telephone to bureaucrats, fellow MPs or people at home in the mountains. The government whip passed his office one day when the bells were giving headaches to the entire human population of Parliament Hill. "Division, Doug," he shouted from the doorway. "Division." Doug waved him away palm forward. "Sorry, couldn't possibly. Much too busy. Far, far too busy."

A year went by before he spoke in the House, another activity for which he saw no need. Conscripted for a debate in some emergency where prepared speakers had failed to show up, Doug told the House of the need for better sewage treatment in the national parks. Two years later, obliged to make a second speech under similar circumstances, he gave the same speech again, ending it with "This is the second time I have brought this to the attention of Honourable Members. I trust it will not be necessary again." He could never recall later the true subject of the debate to which he had contributed oratory. There was no third speech but in the following election, when most of us first-time Liberals from BC were defeated, Doug won re-election.

During that second campaign, his opponent made much of the fact that Doug had placed no questions on the order paper. "He insisted I should be demanding to know the snow removal costs at Cranbrook airport and other arcane statistics which kept civil service staffs occupied if not useful." When re-elected, Doug told his secretary, "If questions on the order paper are what my constituents want, questions on the order paper they shall have." He asked her to find who had placed the most questions on the order paper in the last Parliament and, discovering that it was some Member from Greater Toronto who had not been re-elected, Doug entered his entire stock of unanswered order paper questions. Not one of the questions had any relevance to the people of Okanagan–Kootenay but, as Doug said, that didn't matter, they wanted questions asked and he was the man to supply them. At one point a delegation from External Affairs came to his office and asked, as a special favour, if he would withdraw one of the questions, which, they said, would require the services of seven hundred maids with seven hundred mops for seventy years to answer. He graciously consented to do so but, never having seen the question, he couldn't remember later which one it was and they had to petition him a second time.

The rest of us had no such clear understanding of the parliamentary process and remained awed by the fact that the aisle between the government and opposition benches is of a width such that two men with rapiers cannot touch their tips across it. Breaking the maiden was a prospect that haunted many of us. We took what comfort we could from old John Diefenbaker. "When you come to Parliament on your first day you wonder how you ever got here. After that, you wonder how the other 263 members got here." I spoke during the 1968 budget debate to a House that had a bare quorum of 20 members present out of the 264 who then formed the Commons. I was rewarded by a pleasant note from a cabinet minister who was there that night but even more rewarded by the House of Commons police constable who had heard me from the lobby and when I went out said, "A very strong speech, Mr. St. Pierre." Not a nice speech, not a good speech, a strong speech. Who could ask more from a man who in the normal course of his duties heard a hundred times more speeches than he wanted to listen to? The only other time I felt as good was when the entire House applauded my vote on the Arctic sovereignty issue, a matter in which I had led a two-year caucus revolt.

Both seemed immensely important events at the time. In retrospect, neither mattered much, nothing mattered much and the Parliament itself didn't matter much. The Canadian public had not abandoned the democratic system to the extent this has happened in the United States, where only half the electorate bother voting for a president and barely a third go to the polls for congressional elections, but by century's end Canadians also were absenting themselves from the process, and among those who professed an interest in the subject, a smaller portion of Canadians joined political parties than in the US. It wasn't that people had found a better system, they hadn't, but in the last half of the century most people changed their view of government.

In the heady, in many ways unusually happy days just after the war, a good portion, probably a clear majority of Canadians, saw government as a force for change and improvement of our lot. We hadn't yet found the perfect political formula nor could we agree entirely on which was the perfect party but we were sure that once we cleared up those details, our government would be forever our friend and protector. By century's end, we had come to the conclusion that our main opponent in life was our government, an attitude best summed up by a Chilcotin rancher whose line cabin burned to the ground in mysterious circumstances. "Do you have any enemies?" the police asked. "Can you think of anybody who wants to do you harm?" A quiet man by nature, he thought for a time and then said, "Only the government."

At least half the people in Canada, including at least one high school teacher in my riding, didn't know the difference between parliament and government, and probably even fewer can make this rudimentary distinction today.

The national disinterest didn't seem to bother us MPs much, and I recall when the Member for Sault complained to me that he had held an important constituency meeting and only eighteen people had showed up, I knew the answer all veteran Members had at their hand: "That's six more than attended the Last Supper and they had a bigger draw than you."

Most of us had a sense of high adventure and surging emotions, which of course matter much more in political life than mere facts. We were screwed up so tight we squeaked. I remember, walking Ottawa's streets late at night on my way home to a sleeping room in an elderly lady's house in Rockcliffe (she liked

MPs and also was blessed with a hollow leg that enabled her to drink me under the table), as I was walking home, the smells of childhood came back. I was carried back in memory to scuffing chestnut leaves on Fairbanks Street in Dartmouth, Nova Scotia, as I walked home from Synod Hill School in the chill of November. Everything—sights, smells, sounds—seemed more intense than before I was elected.

That the rest of the world did not realize this, that on our weekly or semi-monthly flights home we used to tell the stewardesses we were Tupperware salesmen because that impressed them more, somehow didn't matter. Nowhere else, not even as a shiny new eighteen-year-old Air Force recruit, had I found myself in such strange surroundings among such awesome, almost godlike people who had arrived before me.

I was also infected by the great Ottawa time-eating-monster virus. No days were long enough for the duties to be done. Most of us arrived at 9 a.m. and left at 10 p.m. We flew home to family and constituents Friday and returned usually Sunday on what we called the Cardiac Special, which left Vancouver last thing at night and arrived at Ottawa in the dawn. More than once I went through security checks and walked to the very gates of the Cardiac Flight, turned, apologized to the attendants and went to a hotel for sleep, taking one of the more civilized flights next day and arriving usually to discover I had failed to keep an appointment.

This general weariness seldom left me for the full four and a half years of that Parliament and looking back, it's regrettable that almost all the time I spent was wasted, although sometimes in interesting ways. If I be a little strange or even slightly mad, I am not alone or unique among those elected to our House of Commons, where, it has been said, the boundary between eccentricity and psychosis has never been clearly delineated.

The purpose of a parliament, for those who still mistake it for government, is to speak. That's what the word means. For most of history in the British tradition, individuals who represented their voters instead of their party did exactly that. The later introduction of the party system, a necessary evil, weakened the system and may well destroy it, but we had little time to think about the currents and riptides of history. Even those of us who rather enjoyed speaking did it rarely for the most part. Orators were few, the exception being the Québécois of all the parties, oratory being a subject still taught in their school system. For a few, speaking exercised a horrid fascination. One who comes to mind—his identity is unimportant—was a small, grey Progressive Conservative who had been told by somebody that he was there to speak and that he failed his constituency and his country if he failed to do so on every occasion on every subject. He occupied a seat on the backbench. His party had backed him up against the lobby curtains, hoping, I suppose, he would learn to duck behind them and leave the House to its business. For all occasions he would arrive carrying sheets of paper on which he had scratched out all his thoughts, which were few and which he delivered with every cliché known to the English-speaking world. His voice was a monotone, never rising or falling by a single decibel.

The fascinating feature was not that these were speeches of excruciating banality—there were a few others in the House who could equal him in stupefying boredom. The extraordinary thing was that he took immense satisfaction in his performance. He was a tone-deaf man singing at the Metropolitan Opera, explaining in some way to himself the strange fact that nobody ever shouted bravo or threw roses at him. Like the world's worst poet or the world's worst actor, he was sublimely confident and, even without the benefit of applause, convinced of his own merit. He probably had merit, much merit, most parliamentarians did, but his was not oratory. Somewhere, I suppose, he sits rereading those long sentences of his, droning like a piper preparing for a tune on the bagpipes without ever launching into a melody. I have not the slightest notion of what he said, ever. Possibly I would have agreed with every word, although I suspect those words were like the Platte River of Nebraska, six inches deep and a mile wide. Like everybody else in the House I let the words wash over my head while seeking something to occupy my time — reading, writing letters to constituents or arranging meetings of the Save the Lemming Society.

The name was chosen because of the habit of these little rodents to swarm at regular intervals and sometimes jump into the ocean and drown. There could be no more appropriate model for Members of Parliament. I chose the name and solicited the first members, although I cannot clearly remember how. I was probably half-cut. We invited Lemming candidates to give us a five dollar bill and, if asked why we wanted five dollars, we answered, "None of your business." Those who paid anyway were considered stupid enough to be Lemmings and joined us one or two times a year for gourmet white spring salmon, prairie oysters, Lake Huron spring smelts and other delicacies. We held these soirees in a private room off the parliamentary library where we invited guest speakers to be harassed unmercifully by half-drunk Lemmings. One of our members, a cabinet minister, aroused everyone's awe by passing unnoticed and unremarked through the crowded parliamentary restaurant proper with four bottles of Scotch concealed on his person, and he was a small man in a close-fitting business suit. He had learned how to do it in the Air Force, where so many of us learned about real life in the 1940s. The Army was never as good as air crew training; all the Army taught was how to open a beer bottle on your belt buckle.

All three major parties of that parliament were represented and every Lemming had a title. Mine was Permanent First Secretary. This was close to Stalin's time and we knew there was no office higher. We weren't too shabby a crew. Five of the thirteen later became judges, another became Speaker of the House, another headed a major Canadian brokerage house, yet another became a Canadian representative in London, England, and I became a police commissioner.

I can recall no more typical nor better guest speaker than Tommy Douglas, prizefighter, Baptist minister, CCF premier of Saskatchewan and at the time of this Lemming dinner leader of the New Democratic Party in the House. Tommy, our very own baptized Godless Red, possessed a superb quality, a brilliant sense of humour. Humour was not uncommon among members of the CCF and the NDP successor party, but he displayed it publicly and often, while the rest considered it dangerous stuff and doled it out sparingly to the public. He was a rare anecdotalist as well as being a complete political realist.

When he was our guest he told of his immense triumph when, back in the '30s, he went to the Green Chamber as the youngest Member ever elected. In 1936, during the first budget debate he ever attended, the Liberal finance minister, Dunning, walked across the floor, sat beside him and said he rather liked a proposal in Tommy's speech. He was prepared to accept an amendment, if Tommy would be good enough to keep the rude criticism of his party out of it. "Willing? I would have put up a notice favourable to Dunning on the Peace Tower." For a fledgling Opposition MP to amend a government budget does happen, but not much oftener than the Queen has twins. He couldn't wait for the capital city papers to blazon his name next day but raced to the train, in those days the only transport available, that he might be among the people of his riding who, he felt, could claim a share of the glory for electing him.

"I didn't expect they'd have time to get a brass band there but I knew there'd be a good crowd and I thought of my wife, who would be so embarrassed about the encomiums of praise being heaped upon me." His speech in response, he felt, might depart far enough from a studiously developed modesty to use some words from Homer: "Much have I seen and known.../ And drunk delight of battle with my peers..."

When he got home it was late at night and the snow was blowing. There was nobody to meet him at the station. After a while a taxi showed up. He flagged it. "Who should the driver be but the man who had been my campaign manager. He said, 'Hi, Tommy. What are you doing here? We all thought you'd gone down to Ottawa.'"

By the time he was a guest, we Lemmings had learned a few simple truths about our lack of importance in the great lack of a grand scheme of things that is Ottawa. A party that gathered in its new boys early in each new parliament and told them about the birds and bees would be, I am sure, richly rewarded by more effective Members. None, to my knowledge, ever seriously undertakes such instruction; rather one senses a feeling among veteran Members that it's best the new people learn the hard way, which might be all right except that some never do.

Part of what made the capital city so strange a place was that realities diverged so far from what we thought we knew to be the case. So many things — the important things — the newspapers never told us. That included my own newspaper, of which I once thought myself to be a knowledgeable editor. The Ottawa press gallery was best known for being the Ottawa press gallery. It had become a sort of senate of the Canadian newspaper business where faithful servants were sent as a reward for long service, there being an unspoken agreement that they need never work again. One of the unkinder critics of my acquaintance compared them with a type of sea limpet in which, once it has found a rock and attached itself to it, the brain withers and disappears because it is no longer needed. The press gallery attended question period although, even in that poor substitute for true debate, few of them trusted their own ears and waited until the Hansard reporters provided them with a preliminary stenographic report called the blues to find out what had happened. It was never clear to me how the rest of their days were spent.

Yet I doubted there were many places of importance in the nation where secrets were less secure than in Ottawa. A characteristic of almost all politicians was an astonishing carelessness about what they said and where. You may call it frankness and be happy about it only if you consider frankness a virtue instead of a lack of skill. Of course, we are all different. Most of my life I have been anxious that people around me should not know what I did or thought, so here in the nation's capital I was frequently horrified to find taxi drivers knew more government secrets than I did.

There is no better example than my own experience at the conclusion of my caucus revolt that resulted in the Arctic Pollution Control Zone legislation. The government was doubtful that this law would withstand a challenge from the Americans at the International Court of Justice at The Hague so it planned to introduce in the House, twenty minutes ahead of the legislative bill, a reservation to be sent to the court, a procedure by which a country can properly announce that it will not submit to court judgment. In this case we did so on the basis that since no body of international law had developed in this field, the court lacked precedents from which a proper judgment could be rendered. The manoeuvre required total secrecy, up to the moment it was introduced in the Commons, and when it was presented the Opposition, who were later to unanimously support the Control Zone legislation, were surprised and puzzled by the announcement.

Among the few people who knew in advance, I was one of the very few outside the cabinet. This came about when the prime minister, vacationing at the Whistler ski resort, calmly outlined the entire strategy at an evening meal. Next morning in Ottawa one of his senior staff phoned me, unsure whether to plead with me or find some way of threatening instant execution. Obviously as the rebel who had done most to bring it into being, I had every interest in leaking the story to some favoured newspaperman. He didn't know about my inhibitions. I told him not to worry and as a reward I was given the original bill as a souvenir, signed by the cabinet, and have it still in some of those cardboard cases of files that I shall probably never sort.

Pierre Trudeau was reckless to place such a trust in me or any other ambitious Member of Parliament. Were I in his position, I would certainly not have been as trusting as he was. Perhaps if I had remained in politics I would have become, like the veterans, strangely incautious but, perhaps, more likeable. The phenomenon seems worldwide. The senior security officer at the United Nations once complained to me about the porosity of all state secrets. One reason, he said, was the delegates' habit of talking about state secrets while riding in taxis in a city where one in five of the drivers had criminal records.

It is, therefore, the exception rather than the rule when secrets are kept, but it produces some touching stories. One was the Unstained Champion story told me circa 1970 at The Hague by Lord Crathorne, like myself a delegate to the NATO Parliamentary Assembly. In some manner, the bitter enmity of Winston Churchill and Stanley Baldwin had arisen in the course of our conversation. Crathorne, before becoming an elected MP, a cabinet minister and eventually a peer of the realm, had been a confidential secretary to Prime Minister Baldwin.

"As you recall," he said (I didn't, of course), "Baldwin left Winston out of his cabinet in 1935 and Winston never forgave him. I remember that on the night Baldwin announced his cabinet appointments, we were alone, and he said to me, 'You know, the hardest thing for me to do in forming this government was to leave out Winston.' So I said, 'Sir, why did you leave him out?' Baldwin said, 'Within ten years, this country will be at war with Germany. Everybody associated with me in this government will be discredited. At that time, the British people have got to have an unstained champion to whom they can turn, and that man may well be Winston Churchill.'"

"Did you never tell this to Churchill?" I said.

He drew himself up in that way English peers sometimes do. "I was a *confidential* secretary," he said, emphasizing the operative word. Then he paused. "Well," he said. "Well. Well. Well, many years later when Baldwin was dying of cancer I had a conversation with the prime minister and as a result the two men were reconciled at Baldwin's bedside the night before he died." In the ancient Knight's Hall of the Netherlands' parliament buildings, I could feel the ghosts of old politicians crowding in to listen to the story of the Unstained Champion.

Committee work caught my attention early in my few years in Parliament, partly because the House was so stultifyingly dull. Practically all speeches were set pieces, the position of every party being well known and the ultimate vote as certain as sun-up. A typical debate would see only one of the hundred or so reporters in the gallery, the representative of the Canadian Press, which had an obsession about keeping a reporter in the chamber. On the floor would be a single cabinet minister on House duty, sometimes two if the minister involved in the legislation wanted to listen and beyond that about twenty members. Twenty was a House quorum without which it could not legally act, but membership often fell below this number and only occasionally would some troublemaker call quorum, whereupon a dozen members who had been smoking behind the curtains, sending a blue cloud into the chamber throughout the day, would scurry into their seats and restore proper numbers.

The press and most of the MPs who were on the Hill that day would attend question period, which was not, properly speaking, a part of parliamentary business but a custom that had grown up over many years and which, by its brevity and occasionally by its wit, provided spark to the chamber and occasionally flame. This too, however, had degenerated into predictable ritual. The 28th Parliament began with the Opposition attacking the government in question period with having failed to do something or other for one side in the civil war in Nigeria, a place where none of us had been and which few could have located rapidly on a map. There was at that time a civil war between the Ibos, who were Christians, and the majority group, who were Muslim. The Christians had hired an excellent public relations firm in New York that had inculcated a widespread public sentiment that the war should be brought to a peaceful conclusion by the Ibos winning.

Few activities seemed to me quite so futile as a Canadian Parliament going to war for one religion against another in a land far, far away. In holding that view, I may have been influenced by the late unlamented Cardinal Spellman of Boston, who had been a key mover in engaging the United States in defending Catholicism against the Godless Reds in Vietnam, where American casualty lists now climbed with every month that passed. I knew one thing: I had better things to do with my time, and I soon developed the habit of rising, bowing to Mr. Speaker and quitting the chamber at the first question about Nigeria, certain that there was work at the office worth more time and attention than this. I never found myself mistaken in that expectation, even if I did nothing but pick numbers at random out of a Williams Lake phone book and ask constituents, usually surprised ones, what they thought of the shape and direction of the national policies.

Committee work was better. It was more informal. We smoked at our places around the perimeter of the committee table instead of ducking behind curtains. We had some power to amend bills that came before us, the right to question witnesses who were brought before us and a considerable power to initiate studies of our own. Committees were and are, I believe, Parliament's last, best hope, but none have the wide-ranging authority of committees of the American Congress or Germany's Bundestag, which is what they should have.

However, any control of the budget was far beyond their capacity. Nobody grasps that subject. Government budgets are now in the billions and the trillions. Do you understand how much a billion is? Neither do I. Nobody does. We humans know how to write the figures, just as we know how to spell the word *God*, but true understanding of either is light-years beyond the capacity of the human brain. We can say (and prove) that the twentieth century lasted only thirty-one and a half trillion seconds, thirty-one and a half billion by the British counting system, but these are mere calculations.

Therefore committee debates about spending, which were often quite fierce, had to focus on fifty- and hundred-thousand-dollar items which, being at the level of the mortgage on many private homes, was a comprehensible figure. In Fisheries and Oceans committee one day I made a note that we had spent almost forty minutes debating the loss of a five-thousand-dollar grant to a Lunenburg fishermen's celebration but had passed the general departmental budget of several hundred million dollars in three and a half minutes.

Once again, we find that the human brain, doubtless the most marvellous creation of the universe, remains hampered by those recent memories of the days when we were in the trees swinging by our tails. Of what possible value to our ancestors was a knowledge of millions and billions of anything, even rocks? Crows, it is said, can count as far as three; beyond that number the bird registers the number as being many. Probably *Pithecanthropus erectus* had the same limitation at about twelve or twenty. Huge numbers are beyond our ken, not only in finance but in more important areas. Stalin, who shipped tens of millions of his citizens away to their deaths, was a man with a proven grasp of essential knowledge. He once said that a single death was a tragedy but the death of a million was merely a statistic.

The intelligence of government, once it grows beyond small-town size, is seldom impressive. Large government experiences great difficulty in associating cause with effect. It seldom learns by experience. In the 1920s both Canada and the United States launched what was called the noble experiment of prohibiting alcohol, one of the most damaging of mind-altering substances. They achieved the creation of immense criminal empires and revoked Prohibition before Al Capone could become president. With this example before them, both governments proceeded to conduct an even costlier war on narcotic drugs, with the result that even bigger criminal empires were created and no section of society, practising politicians, police or such services as the Central Intelligence Agency could avoid having some of its membership seduced into the criminal sale and transport of narcotics. A cat learns the peril of sitting on a hot stove only once and never forgets, but governments are not so clever.

Thus the same familiar problems recur for every government of every party of every parliament. Poverty: whatever the current measurement may be, there is too much of it. The price of Prairie wheat. Too many fishermen chasing too few fish. The dominance of the American colossus and that ever popular girl Laura Norder. The problems come around as regularly and as predictably as the horses of the merry-go-round and each government offers solutions to those problems which, it knows, are endemic and enduring and are never going to be solved by anyone. The poor, the unhappy, the unfortunate ye shall have with you always. What is it about politics that instead of offering what comfort there may be we insist that there is a solution to the unsolvable and that ours is the only government that knows the secret?

For the ordinary Member, outside government and sent to Ottawa ostensibly to talk of many things during the months between harvest and planting, as the original parliamentary schedule went, the power to execute actions for public good or general development is almost zero. When it does fleetingly exist there is a peculiar ambivalence to it.

In the spring of 1973 a couple of Coast–Chilcotin residents, whom I shall not identify too closely, were desperate for a drug needed by their desperately ill child. The situation was life-or-death for the youngster, and supplies of the drug in Canada, if not in the whole world, had not come up to demand level. They asked me to intercede on their behalf. I did. They got the drug. When the election came, my second one, which I lost, the parents wanted to go public in praise of their MP, lifesaver and friend. I said no way; it was never mentioned.

There were any number of good reasons for not using the case in a political campaign or, indeed, in any public way, and they are selfish, not noble. First, I have no idea whether my intercession made the slightest difference in the matter. I would prefer to believe that the life-or-death decision was made on some sounder basis of choice than a letter from a politician. Yet it would have been unthinkable for me to refuse to write on their behalf. If I had not and some other MP or other public figure did so for a different child, the blame might be directly mine. On the other hand, assume that my plea on the child's behalf tipped the scales in his favour. If that were so, somewhere was another child in Canada whom I had condemned to death, a power that should not have been mine. None of this could I explain to the parents, who had troubles enough in their lives, and the matter faded away so completely that most of the details are completely lost to memory; what remains is that it was one of the awful weights you accumulated as a politician and carried always with you.

My defeat in my second campaign, which was a narrow one, a dozen votes, may indeed have been sought by me. Native Indians have a theory that the hunter does not hunt the game, the prey seeks the hunter, and this may well be true in politics. There is a constant drain of not only one's physical and emotional energy. One awakes in the morning tired and goes to bed, a bit drunk, more tired. Subconsciously, the mind seeks rest and recognizes that a political defeat is the way to obtain that rest. Some pundits have never understood why US President Gerald

Ford threw away so many crucial votes in a televised debate by announcing, out of the blue, so to speak, that there was much freedom in Poland, which was then in the grip of an iron Communist dictatorship. It was wrong, and gratuitously wrong, so why did he say it? Mr. Ford may not have known the answer himself but it was probably his subconscious seeking the peace of political defeat.

Looking back today, had those dozen votes gone the other way it is very doubtful I would be alive today. I was overweight and undermuscled. Although I told people I drank only a bottle of whisky a day I knew that it was more than that. (You can tell when you are into heavy drinking: you don't have hangovers any more and you are never drunk although also never completely sober.) My marriage, which had been a happy one for many years, was almost over. I had sold my house for $45,000 and in the rising real estate market could get only a poor substitute for $75,000 in 1973. That was then sold to facilitate the divorce settlement and for some years I had no house of my own.

I interject here that not all MPs are such bad managers. One of my fellow MPs—being a socialist he had a keener appreciation of capitalism than I did—hocked himself to the eyeballs to buy a house in Ottawa the week he got there, invited other MPs to live there and pay the mortgage for him and, at the end of four years, had doubled his money. I blame no one for my financial situation; I merely state the facts of my own case. All my savings were gone and I was in debt, debts that I did not finally pay off until a year after losing that election. Even at that I was much luckier than some long-serving Members of Parliament. More than one told me that there was no hope of them ever escaping the pit of debt they had dug for themselves and in which they would die. They had abandoned all hope of ever again being solvent.

When the MPs of the 28th voted themselves a pay raise, I was among the simon-pure who spoke against it and refused to accept it. I was irritated a bit, still am, by the hypocrites who said, "Gosh, it's wrong to stick the public this way but I must go along with a democratic decision." Speaking in the House in opposition to the raise, I recounted the story of Vancouver mayor Gerry McGeer, an occasional tosspot, who came home after a long bender bearing whisky in his arms. He told his long-suffering wife that it had been supplied him by the family doctor. "Every four hours, I am to take a glass of it. It may be, my dear, that when it is time for me to take this awful stuff I shall be sleeping. If I am sleeping, wake me and if I won't take it, make me." The House was not amused. I was not the only one to refuse the pay raise (an act which hypocrites claim cannot be done, but can, quite easily). I acted quite simply on the basis that we all knew what the pay was when we ran for office and none of us had told the voters we wanted more during the campaign. Of the four others who refused the raise, of whom I have knowledge, not one was returned to the next parliament. The back steps of Parliament are filled with principled MPs.

The final act of my political career was in the sudden snap election of '80 when the Conservative prime minister, possibly in the grip of the death wish of which I speak, had arranged his defeat on a money bill in the House. I had hoped to run again, but not until I had recuperated and made some more money. I announced my non-candidacy and attended a nomination meeting in the coastal town of Sechelt, where there were representatives from exactly half of the riding, which was about half the size of France and reached inland more than halfway to Alberta.

There were two main contenders for the candidate's role and after two ballots, one was elected by a vote of 61 to 60 or 91 to 90. I remember that the margin was a single vote.

A week later the BC Liberal party president phoned me to say that the losing contender had not been happy about losing by one vote. "She insisted that the party check the credentials of all those voting. So, okay, we did. Paul, guess what we found."

"What?"

"We found she had a case. There was one person there voting who was not a paid-up member of the Liberal Party. Now you're only allowed one guess who that person was."

"Oh shit," I said.

"With a gold star on it and a silk ribbon tied around," she said.

I don't know how she managed it, but the nomination stood without another vote being held. It's one of those clever things that get done in politics. In the election that followed, the man who replaced me as Liberal candidate won, as almost certainly I could have, and my children told me that my wife, from whom I was then separated, wept as she watched the television news on election night. I have not taken out any party memberships since then. I almost ran for the Libertarians in 2000, although I was not then nor have I ever been a member of that party.

JUDGES ARE FROM MARS

SOMEHOW IT'S ALWAYS THE SAME STORY when the Martians come visiting. They kidnap some farmer from his sugar beet field, take him for a ride in their spaceship, give him an anal probe and return him a day or so later. You wonder about these alien ways. Why don't they give anal probes to the prime minister, the governor of the Bank of Canada or some of the other movers and shakers in Ottawa?

There is an explanation, which is that the Martians have visited Ottawa also and have had dealings with the leaders of the nation. Some of them are still there, having been appointed to the Supreme Court of Canada. Only people as alien to our customs and culture as Martians could make decisions such as some of that court's in the past decade.

A few examples will serve.

At one point the court threw out a criminal case because the authorities had been slow in prosecuting it. Few could quarrel with that decision. Most would see it as a very belated acknowledgement of the ancient legal principle that justice delayed is justice denied. It's what followed that is so curious.

Naturally every ambulance chaser in Canada began pleading prosecution delays and other murderers, child molesters and rapists went their merry way to freedom. Could it be that the problem of court backlogs was going to be solved by so many cases being thrown out that there would be judges enough to handle the rest speedily?

It was then that we saw the curious break with tradition. A Supreme Court justice, visiting Britain, took the occasion of distance from home to make a speech that might perhaps be read by Canadian lawyers but not the Canadian public. He told the Brit audience that what the Supreme Court of Canada really meant to say in its original judgment was not exactly what was being understood. Out the window and into the backyard trash went one of the oldest of old court traditions—that every judgment speaks for itself and cannot be subject of explanation later. It ranks with another ancient tradition, "Let justice be done though the heavens fall." Few expected such traditions to perish in the twentieth century, even momentarily.

A little later came Supreme Court Madam Justice Claire L'Heureux-Dubé, who made another speech in which she made it clear that she felt homosexuals had not had a fair shake in this land, which may be true, and that she intended to redress the balance with her decisions, which is plainly outrageous. One can only assume she was carried away with the heady feeling of power that goes with the new position of judges in Canada, in which they make law in addition to defining it.

There has been more, much more alien influence in our highest court. It has ruled that some Canadians are more equal than others, finding that the equality provisions of the Canadian Charter of Rights and Freedoms have more application to some groups of society than to others and that the others need not apply for relief under its provisions.

This sort of thing has trickled down into the lower levels of the judiciary, as might be expected. In Vancouver a Supreme Court judge dismissed charges against a man for sexual fondling of a three-year-old child because the child had made advances to the man. Improper advances, we must conclude.

Finally on this scene came a president of the BC Bar Association to offer a comment that, it is generally believed, added very little to the theory or practice of the justice system. The bar association president warned that if criticism of judges was going to be accepted, the public might well become critical of them. Later a Supreme Court of Canada justice said much the same—no criticism, please, it leads to criticism.

Such fatuous talk aroused little comment in Canada. If anyone had suggested that the prime minister, the mayor or, for that matter, the head of the local chapter of the Imperial Order of the Daughters of the Empire should be shielded from criticism lest she be criticized, there would have been at the least a roar of laughter from one coast to another. Judges, it seems, are different.

In a sense, they are. Traditionally they were exempt from public criticism because it was unfair—tradition forbade them answering. That was, however, before they entered the political arena, willingly or not, and began pontificating on what laws should be instead of interpreting what they are. They always had the power to dismiss some pieces of legislation, usually because of questions of federal or provincial jurisdiction, sometimes because of a violation of natural justice as provided by our old common law, the Magna Carta being one of the noted examples. But when Canada patriated the Constitution and then rewrote it with the Charter of Rights and Freedoms, the remaking of laws became more frequent. In recent years almost a third of the cases before the Supreme Court of Canada have involved Charter challenges. As a result, some laws passed by the democratically elected Members of Parliament have been altered or rejected holus-bolus by some old, unelected men and women who are secure in their positions of power until age 75 unless they rape their secretaries on the courthouse steps at high noon, without using condoms.

Something went very wrong with our politicians that they handed over so many of their powers to these remote members of the ruling class. Which is as good a time as any to say that I am one of the politicians who favoured such action and, had I been in Parliament at the time, would have voted for it. Never mind all those other people, who are so often wrong, how did *I* go so wrong?

Perhaps for me politics and the judiciary came together during a lunch at 26 Sussex Drive in 1968. Pierre Elliott Trudeau, then in his first term, made a practice of lunching with groups of backbench members of the 28th Parliament. It was supposed to be so we would all get to know one another better. There wasn't much progress. Nobody ever got to know Pierre Trudeau well. He was one of the most solitary of men by nature. It was said that he never spent a full night with a woman during his bachelor years but would always, in the small hours, dress and go home to his own bed. The tendency to be a loner was accentuated, of course, when he became prime minister. All prime ministers are required to be loners. A prime minister can have few intimate friends and none within his cabinet. The operation of government requires that every member of a cabinet be subject to instant dismissal, both for good reasons and for bad reasons. Friendships interfere with the ability to sometimes sacrifice good men for what seems to be, at the time, a higher good. So Mr. Trudeau had no true passion to know and be known by us backbenchers. Even by prime ministerial standards, he was independent of all about him. He was one of the toughest hombres, on himself as well as on others, that I ever knew.

However, from his university days he retained a taste of intellectual exercises, asking hard and intricate questions and examining the answers with his cold, Cossack eyes. On this occasion, when half a dozen of us were dining feebly on delicate fish, white asparagus and good cold wines, he offered us a challenge. "You fellows have time to think. I seem to be too busy all the time for thinking. Why don't you write me about your ideas for how Parliament might be restructured?" He had made it clear he didn't think either Parliament or government was functioning well. They weren't, but then, they never have.

No doubt he was sincere in inviting us to write him essays, provided we had a point to make and made it clear and fast. He could be merciless when confronted with platitudes or cant. Anything written for him would have to be short, original and free of the kind of jargon favoured by academics. Although he was an academic himself he frequently showed a contempt for them and more than once in caucus dismissed some professor's public argument with "After all, he's only an academic."

His invitation was attractive, and I don't doubt every one of us new boys went back to the Hill that day determined to write a new constitution for the nation. I didn't do it. I doubt that any of us did. Only people who have been on the Hill realize how the hours of every day fill up and spill over into the night hours. New MPs have even less time than old MPs. Writing constitutional ideas was a tomorrow job and tomorrow can never be today.

There is no doubt what I would have written. There is little doubt what the others thought. Almost certainly we would have urged more power to the Canadian Supreme Court to enforce constitutional rights. It seemed so abundantly clear. That should have warned us off. The abundantly clear is wrong more often than it is right.

We were influenced powerfully by the American Supreme Court. In the 1960s it had accomplished what a century of politicians had failed to accomplish. It had brought justice and a considerable measure of equality to the American black people. What better recommendation could there be for courts and constitutions?

A pity that I and others never paused to consider the record of the United States Supreme Court in such matters, because for one and a half centuries it had been a powerful instrument of oppression for 10 percent of the American people. It had roused itself to decent behaviour just a bit ahead of the majority of the nation's politicians. A minority of those politicians had always been in advance of their Supreme Court in pursuit of justice for black people.

It was this court that declared that the testimony of one white man was equal in credibility to the testimony of two blacks. By the infamous Dred Scott decision, it had ruled that a black man was not an American citizen. These and other monstrous rulings by the nation's top judges far outweighed the powers of the Senate and House of Representatives because the word of the court was the word of God. Every court in the land was obliged to accept procedures that identified black people as inferior human beings, possessed of fewer rights than the whites. Minor judges could not debate this, as might be done in Congress. They were obliged to accept it, no matter what their personal convictions. The members of the Supreme Court were as unfair and as prejudiced by nature as the majority of the people in Congress during those long, dreadful decades of slavery followed by near slavery, but the court, because of its position, could entrench injustice more solidly than elected people could.

If anyone needed evidence of the harm that can be done by too powerful a court, there was no need to look farther than Washington, DC. Yet we MPs, gullible as most people, looked there and learned the opposite lesson. The fact that the American Supreme Court had repented somehow obliterated our view of its actions from 1775 to 1950, a rather considerable slice of history. That is an ailment endemic in electoral politics. Whether examining the past or the future, all thinking is short-term thinking. The politician's mind does not extend far into the future or into the past. He lives in a continuous present, and in that present of the late 1960s the power of a high court to do good shone out, brightly enough to cause temporary legislative blindness.

Elsewhere in this book I argue that democracy is a tricky instrument and that ordinary men and women need some extra protection against the tyranny of a majority, which the brilliant Alexis de Tocqueville so clearly anticipated in the great American democratic experiment. So if there must be some guarantees, where else to get these than from our courts? How can I criticize the unbridled power of judges while casting doubt on the ability of elected people to be just and fair?

Yes, courts are needed for that role, but there are other places where citizens' rights can be safeguarded. A functioning Senate would be one. But if the main reliance is to be upon courts, and probably it must be, let us never forget that these people are unelected guardians. In the near future the best we can do is to introduce the American system of electing our judges. If their role is to be partly legislative, let them stand for office and let us do our best not to repeat here such things as the election of Senator Joe McCarthy to a judgeship in his native state. In the longer term we should rewrite that hasty pudding Constitution and clearly make it the duty of judges to define the statutes the elected people write. Those who depend upon election may become haughty, arrogant or careless, but they can never forget completely that votes count.

Having said all this, it may seem absurd or at least quaint for me to note that one of my best friends was a judge. He died several years ago. I miss him to this day and always will. If my criticism of the judicial system now seems absurd, then so be it. Criticism is what is intended.

I go further. Over half a century I became acquainted with many judges at all levels, from police courts to supreme and appeal courts. I never met one who didn't arouse admiration and respect in me. They are almost always, intellectually and morally, a superior lot. But they must not be excepted from the one general rule that should apply top to bottom in any society — never give any more power to any man than you can help. Lord Acton said, "Power tends to corrupt and absolute power corrupts absolutely." More important, he went on to say, "Great men are almost always bad men."

It's not great men or powerful men that the nation needs, it is good men, common sense men. I think with some joy of a stipendiary magistrate who presided over the little courtroom in the almost invisible village of Quesnel long years ago. He was presented with a case under the BC Surveyors' Act. A retired naval officer had run a fenceline for a neighbouring rancher, using some optical instrument from his ship. The act forbade any layman to peer through a surveyor's instrument for that purpose, thus preserving the integrity and the income of the survey profession. The question was: was a naval optical instrument a survey instrument for the purpose of the act? Today a posse of lawyers would argue this up and into that ugly old Supreme Court apple box building in Ottawa. Not then. Not in Quesnel. The stipendiary magistrate ruled, "You ain't exactly guilty, strictly speaking. But you came so goddamn close that I am goin' to fine you anyhow." The retired naval officer paid $25. Everybody in Quesnel knew the stipendiary magistrate was not from Mars.

Common Man's Best Friend: A King or Queen

Unless the legend makers have it wrong, and that does happen, Siam chose its first king from twelve of the nation's finest young men who were lined up in the throne room, naked as jaybirds. Six deep-throated bronze gongs regulated the process. When the first sounded, twelve dwarfs marched into the room, stationed themselves each before a candidate and painted honey on his belly. At another gong, they left and were replaced by twelve other dwarfs who released flies, which settled on the honey. They left, again there was a gong, and twelve more dwarfs marched in and positioned themselves behind each candidate. The fourth gong brought in twelve beautiful dancing girls, each of whom removed her clothing, a bit at a time, in front of each candidate, with the result that every man's penis came fully erect. When the fifth gong sounded, each dwarf reached between his candidate's legs, grasped the tumescent penis and pulled it backward. It sounds complicated, but royalty involves formality.

At the final gong the twelve dwarfs released the penises and the man whose penis killed the most flies became king of Siam, a reason that the capital city is called Bangkok.

This is an unusual way to choose a monarch but it probably serves as well as any other. The important thing is not how you select him or even who he is. The important thing is that monarchies are as permanent as institutions get to be in the world.

Kings and queens are not smarter than presidents, dictators and various other heads of state in other nations. It's often the reverse. The good thing about monarchies is that the citizens in them are healthier and happier, an observation that most of us are too slow to make.

Since we began with Siam, let's observe how that monarchy has functioned. Most power in that country shifted to a parliament a long time ago, but it remains a proudly monarchial nation under the name Thailand. One of those anally retentive Englishwomen who give their country a bad name went out to Siam many years ago as governess to the king's children, and she wrote an ill-mannered book about it that described the king as half barbarian and half clown and, worst of all, not an Englishman. History takes a very different view of King Phrachomklao. He was a sophisticated man of high intelligence. During his reign every nation around Siam was being snatched up for colonies by the British and the French. He had no army and no strong economy. Yet, playing in a high-stakes game with scarcely any chips, the king came out the winner and Thailand remains independent to this day, without the bloodbaths that attended Vietnam, Cambodia and Burma. Talleyrand and Metternich would have admired King Phrachomklao. They would have recognized the towering ability an ill-bred woman couldn't perceive.

Circle the world and what do we find in monarchial countries?

Japan, the world's second mightiest nation, hasn't done all that badly under a series of emperors, even if one of them was a certifiable lunatic.

What of Europe? Britain, an economic powerhouse, is a monarchy. So also are the happier nations of that continent — Norway, Sweden, Denmark, the Netherlands and Spain — and the Germans may well ask themselves if their nation was made healthier and happier by getting rid of the foolish old Kaiser.

Australians recently held a plebiscite on whether to retain the monarchy or replace it with a republican system. The ballot was badly worded and the defeat of the plan was narrow, so probably not too much should be read into vote figures. One thing, however, was notable. The monarchy's strongest support came from working-class ridings, where the lower-income Australians made it clear they knew who their champion was and it wasn't Australia's republicans of the chattering classes.

I never expected to end up a monarchist. It is something that came and curled up on my lap while I wasn't paying attention. At twenty I wanted nothing to do with kings and queens. Twenty is a grand age in many respects. You are aware that you don't know everything but you have the comfort of knowing that anything you do not know could not possibly be important. It's different when you are old enough to know better.

Affection doesn't play much part in my conversion. The Queen Mum was an exception, of course. More than any other single person she was the reason we won the Second World War. Also it was hard not to love a woman who, at 100 years of age plus, drank too much mother's ruin, played the ponies, was wildly overdrawn on her bank account because of the ponies and called her son-in-law The Hun. However, the affection I felt for the old lady was an aberration and doesn't extend to the other family members. I suspect Prince Charles would be as dreary a dinner guest as an environmentalist, and his former wife Diana may have been a great one-night stand, but where marriage is concerned I would just as soon bed a python.

All of this merely confirms that the royal family of the House of Windsor or Hanover or Battenberg or whatever is pretty much like families in the houses next door to us. They're good sorts, most of the time, but they also sometimes screw around carelessly, get divorced, have fits of being greedy, selfish, lazy and, in the case of King George III, as crazy as bedbugs. In royalty that is not a weakness, that is strength. Although the royals are always raised in somewhat unusual circumstances, they persist in being ordinary human beings.

Ordinary human beings are what we cannot find by the democratic process we use to form our governments. We send regiments, battalions, nay, whole armies of lawyers into Parliament. The few who aren't lawyers are in some other way elitists, people who know what is best for us and are going to see that we get it good and hard. If the occasional MP goes to Ottawa or, as an MLA, to one of the provincial legislatures as a plain citizen, he soon learns to distance himself from the people who sent him there. Even more haughty and distant from the ordinary people are the mandarins of the bureaucracy, secure in their rich castles in the capital city where the drawbridge is always up.

True, whether Canada, Britain, Norway or any other monarchy, the kings and queens do not govern. "They reign but do not rule" is the standard formula. Yet all of them retain one vital power, a power that makes every cent spent upon them worthwhile. They have the power to select a new ruler when government becomes inoperable.

Don't say governments cannot become inoperable here. What has happened in Russia can happen anywhere and, in time, probably will. Civil chaos and a breakdown of the machinery of government have visited practically every republican state in the world. In some countries, such as France, the breakdown comes two or three times a century. This is when a nation cries out for the monarch's precious royal prerogative to choose the next prime minister and ask him or her to gain the people's confidence in parliament or in a general election. In such terrible times we need a person who got the power to do such choosing by the pure accident of birth, the way almost all of us got here. It is no job for political party people. They would like us to think so, but it isn't. It requires someone who got there not by election, not by cleverness, not by lobbying, not by manipulation of party apparatus or by the spinning of ornate philosophic tapestries. It's a job for an ordinary person, which is really what kings and queens are.

Such a person, one of our own kind, can be expected to choose a leader for the nation in the same way we usually choose candidates when we go to the ballot box, by what the late Bruce Hutchison so wisely called a solid gut instinct.

This capacity to snatch a country from the brink of a precipice is the great, I suggest unanswerable, argument in favour of the institution of hereditary monarchy. To this add the fact that practically every king and queen serves as a daily display of good manners, courtesy and common decency.

However, the right monarch for Canada is not the able and personable Mrs. Elizabeth Battenberg.

We all know that Her Majesty does not grant interviews, not even to her husband, but her representatives in Canada hold less rigid views, and when he was governor general, Roland Michener agreed to be interviewed by Southam's Charlie Lynch. There was a remarkable passage between them during that interview.

Charlie asked what, of the many duties as head of state Mr. Michener performed, could not be performed just as well by the chief justice of the Supreme Court of Canada.

Mr. Michener's answer was immediate. "None," he said. "Not one." The trouble, he said, came later when it was time to replace that chief justice. Who was to do this?

Here His Excellency put the finger on the problem, succession, the problem that besets all dictatorships and some democracies. When a ruler is removed, how do you make a peaceful transition to another ruler? With a presidential system succession has come about all too often with gunfire. British-style parliamentary government accomplishes transitions better than others, probably all the others, but all systems have faults.

Here, if a chief justice of Canada's Supreme Court were to also undertake the duties of head of state, the matter of his appointment would become immensely more important; he would be not only heading the court but also heading the state. How is such an important figure to be selected? If you elect him and call him High Chamberlain, Grand Pooh-bah, Big Toadstool Toad or some other title, you are merely extending the political system, taking power from the parliamentarians and handing it to a man still burdened with the flaws of partisan politics.

196

It may be said that the same flaw is inherent in our system of appointing governors general. However, governors general are appointed for six years, not for a lifetime.

Worse than this, although Governor General Michener did not choose to say it during the interview, the one essential and vital part of a governor general's mandate is to choose a new prime minister in times of chaos. If there is chaos in the nation, be assured it was arranged by the elite and we don't want one of the elite trying to fix it. A chief justice is just about the most elite of all the elitists.

As for our present situation, the governor general acts in the Queen's name but with further complications. He represents the Queen federally, but ten lieutenant-governors represent her provincially. As a result she may end up fighting herself. The system works because we want it to, the best reason for any system to operate.

We are left with this question, however: Who chooses the governor general? Why, the party in power, of course. It may choose well or poorly. It may reward a politician or elevate a businessman or a popular entertainer to six years of viceregal life. This is not and never can be the same as a Canadian hereditary monarch who would come to the throne by being born to it, the one true commoner among the elitists set in authority over us.

If we need this one true commoner, we might as well recognize that Queen Elizabeth, a lady beyond reproach, is not the person for us. Although the English tabloids from time to time like to point out that she is German, this is mere mischief making. If Elizabeth is German then so was John Diefenbaker, and Winston Churchill was an American. By such genealogic trickery it could be proven that not a single Canadian exists or ever did. The Queen is, as every reasonable man and woman knows, English with a dash of Scottish. She will always be closer to what she refers to as "these dear old islands" than she could hope to be to any overseas state. That is no fault. There would be something wrong with the woman if she did not feel so about her own land and people. We ask her to perform royal duties for us and she does. To ask her for affectionate understanding of far-away dominions is like asking a mother to bond to some shirt-tail cousin rather than her own children.

We could and probably should retain the tie with Britain by picking the founder of the Canadian royal house from the royal family. Prince Harry, Charles's second son, seems a lively young fellow and might enjoy the position. There are lots of others. One of the princes of the blood in Britain was harried by London newspapermen recently for snorting cocaine. Any man attacked by the English gutter press must have a lot of good in him. He might make a good king.

If we came up dry in Britain there is that great royal dipping pool in the old kingdoms of Germany. Royals bred like fruit flies in the fourteen princedoms of old Germany and there is always a candidate available for shipment abroad. Or we could pick a Canadian and be surprised how quickly that person would learn to be gracious and kind and able to exhibit a seemingly sincere interest in Mrs. Boutilier's mustard pickle at the Lunenburg Fall Fair.

What could we offer this Canadian king or queen?

In truth, precious little. The present queen, we are told, prayed through all her childhood that her parents would have a baby boy. A few have suggested that in a better and fairer world she might have spent her time among the creatures who matter to her, they being the ones who eat grass and fart. Indeed, some of us would dash out our babies' brains on the cobblestones if we thought they were going to be imprisoned for life in a golden cage, wearing a heavy crown.

This doesn't matter. There are people out there who will do the job. Don't ask why. They are there. Just read history. They can be found.

What would we ask of our monarchs?

Again, little.

We would expect the monarch to have, or acquire, that precious regal trait of grace under pressure. We would want a royal family that displayed standards of decent behaviour, not decent as defined by the priesthood or sociologists but recognizably decent to ordinary men and women, who have a very clear and unobstructed vision in that respect.

If, like other human beings, our royals sometimes did wrong, we would ask them, discreetly, to please do wrong discreetly. We could be confident that they would oblige.

We would require that the royals have children. Without children, where is the permanence? A royal couple unable to produce babies would adopt two or three.

There's not much more.

We could rid them in advance of some of the humbug that attaches to royal houses. Succession would be the oldest child, male or female, of the first royal marriage. (There's no point in expecting royal marriages to be divorce proof; that rule has been abandoned already in London.) We would also make it clear that there is nothing wrong with abdication in cases of debilitating illness or old age.

All royals would need titles but we could quite easily avoid cluttering Canada with aristocrats by adopting an old Chinese system whereby the children of kings and queens drop a level of aristocratic rank with each generation, returning to commoner status within two or three generations.

With good luck, we could develop much affection between the Canadian people and their royals. Even with bad luck, which also comes by the accident of birth, Canadians would still know that they had at least one of their own in Ottawa—the Monarch, First Commoner of the Equal Commoners of Canada, or some other illogic terminology.

THE LAW AND THE REALITY

AT THE MILLENNIUM'S TURN we were still obsessed with the idea of curing human nature and other perceived ailments with laws, police, courts and jails. Reformers formed most of the ruling class and as Finley Peter Dunne's Mr. Dooley so aptly observed, a true reformer cannot sleep at night when he knows there is still one bed vacant in the jailhouse. So, in America, a nation founded on devotion to freedom, there are now usually two million people in prisons at any randomly chosen date. A large proportion are there for using drugs other than alcohol and coffee but some are there by such processes as California's three-strikes law. (The man on sentry duty shouts, "Who goes therethreetimesBANG!") At the time of writing, a Californian has been jailed for life for stealing a slice of pizza. Not the whole pizza, just a slice.

(Most of those jailed are blacks and poor people but let's not get hung up on that, what else would you expect? Blacks and the poor also took the heaviest casualties in Vietnam. Downtrodden people get trodden down, that's what the name means.)

With so many of the wicked and the foolish poor and the blacks tucked out of harm's way, eating the pizza at Hotel Crowbar, the citizens left outside should be remarkably free of crime, anger, sorrow, poverty or the shingles, but no, the criminals are still out here among us and they just keep on breaking more and newer laws as fast as they can be enacted. The state of affairs in the United States is remarkably similar to the situation of England in the days before Robert Peel brought in his famous bobby, who, like the Mounted Police in the Canadian West, proved that you can be a policeman and popular also. For generations, England had had the reputation on the continent of being a dangerous country to visit, just as the United States has today. As in the US, England introduced draconian laws to hang, jail and deport. England hanged fourteen-year-old children for stealing shoe buckles. At the time of the French Revolution, during the Reign of Terror, England was hanging more people than France was sending to the guillotine. With a perversity that is the despair of all those who try to run other people's lives for them, both the English and the American people continued committing crimes until other forces brought about a more peaceable society.

All this is merely to say that simple solutions seldom work. If this chapter contained nothing more than that, it would be scarcely worth paper or ink. What's needed is a reality check.

A reality check during the Terror in Paris, which is possible because the French bureaucrats have preserved all the records, shows that it wasn't aristocrats who were being hauled off in the tumbrels. Yet the French people could well have afforded to lose a bunch of them. To be sure, a few titled folk were beheaded on what was the equivalent of prime time on the TV news. The reality was that most of the people being killed were little shop girls, labourers, fishermen, farmers, ribbon clerks — the real people a country can't afford to lose. Once the French realized that, they shot Robespierre.

England was killing every hangashore in town on the theory let's do something, even if it's wrong. Later Robert Peel and others got it right, and people soon forgot that England had been the crime capital of the world.

What's reality in Canada today?

One reality is that the rulers have completely forgotten one of the army's great common sense laws, which is: Never issue an order that you cannot enforce. The unenforceable order has been issued on narcotic drugs and everybody pays a terrible price for it.

Another reality is that we have blurred the definition of crime and no longer clearly distinguish between good and bad behaviour. Definitions have altered. Nobody is now a criminal until a final court of appeal has agreed that he is, by majority vote. That is the official position: innocent until finally proven guilty after seventeen appeal processes. There is also an unofficial one, which is just the reverse. Everybody is considered to be guilty as charged until he is so found by a jury of his peers, after which he is considered innocent and immense time and effort is spent in trying to avert his punishment.

It follows that if a jury finds you not guilty of stealing $72 million from the widows and orphans in the People's Savings and Loan, then the fact that you have bought three castles on the Rhine on hotdog stand earnings is evidence of the existence of the Tooth Fairy and should not be questioned.

There's another hard reality, one we are still reluctant to accept: today almost every Canadian is a criminal. It's a rare day when you can go from dawn to dark without committing some crime, usually a jailable one. After dark, when the bars are busy, the chances of you remaining law abiding are even less. Most of the time you don't even know what law you are breaking or why it is there or how long it has been there. There isn't a man alive — our most knowledgeable judge, our priciest lawyer — who knows about more than a small percentage of the crimes that the state has invented for us. Ignorance of the law is no excuse. Otherwise those expensive jails would be largely empty.

As is noted elsewhere in this book, whether a crime has been committed and whether a certain individual did it is no longer the central question. The main question is whether the matter is worth pursuing, a bureaucratic decision made in secret.

This substitution of bureaucratic policy for law of the land is even more obvious today when there is unwritten and largely unspoken agreement at the top levels that growing marijuana is all right as long as the Americans don't make too much of a fuss about us shipping a lot of it across the border. Smoking a joint has been effectively legalized for everybody. There have been no recent administrative decisions to prosecute people for that crime.

Then why not change the law, or even abolish it? The sophisticated answer is another question: Why invite political debate, rancour and ill feeling to gain an objective that can be attained by administrative decisions or, better yet, indecisions?

The law may say it is a crime to smoke cannabis. The reality says it is not. Most of us know more realities than we know law.

Law has been taken away from the ordinary people, who could understand murder, robbery and rape, and given to legions of lawyers to conjugate.

If it works, why knock it?

Because it doesn't work all that well, despite the outward signs. When we do not enforce marijuana law, traffic law and a thousand other laws that have gone largely into the discard pile, we encourage a general contempt for all our laws. Also, the ordinary man knows that there is no law or regulation, no matter how absurd, that may not be invoked against him by some coven of witches in a distant government office. The old farmer near Chatham, Ontario, who was fined for shingling his roof without permission, doubtless never imagined that a law had been passed limiting his right to keep the rain out of his living room. It had, and whimsical as ever, the rulers enforced that one.

We may assume he joined the growing number of the disenchanted who now view their country's laws with a mixture of fear and contempt. We have gone a long way down this blind alley and it is dark and dangerous.

Fascism, an Idea Whose Time Has Come

WRITING ON THIS SUBJECT I perceive myself speaking to a great-grandchild who is, this day, becoming officially an adult. In his time that may be the age of 30 or, God help them all, 12. There are enough twelve-year-olds running things here now in 2002. Whatever the age, this is not a subject for children but for those who have begun to wonder how the world runs and how it should.

To this descendant three generations down the timeline I say that I want to tell you something about the parliamentary democratic system of Canada at the time this is committed to print.

That I should not know the system of government my great-grandchildren will know is one of the surprising questions I found to ask myself when I was in my seventies. In my years before 70, I had enjoyed a comfortable unexamined certainty that our system of government, although imperfect, was, as Winston Churchill said, the least imperfect of them all. The future? The future would be like the report of the Veterans Land Act inspector reporting on a farm development. "I see nothing but success ahead for this venture so long as you can keep the stock from shitting in the well." A good and dear friend named Tom Brydon sent me exactly the same advice by post when I was elected to Parliament. I enjoyed what many people did in the closing years of the twentieth century: I had confidence that the system would go on and on with just a bit of patching here and there on the worn spots.

Other people saw that the democratic parliamentary system, like most of the presidential republican systems in the developed world, was in dangerous disarray and eventually, so did I. Most governments had lost the mandate of the people and many had been deserted by the people, none more spectacularly than the government of the United States, where two-thirds of the electors no longer took part in the system of electing their representatives and only one out of two thought it worthwhile to vote for one candidate or another for president. The majority had given up on the system, although, like lapsed Christians going to church with parents, they continued to chant the mantras of faith in democracy.

The loss of faith, the one thing that can give men strength, was first observable to Canadians in the United States, and at this point I pause to describe Americans to you, in case they have changed. Canadians could not have asked for better people to live next door. They were generous, sturdy and by training and nature helpful.

For a reason lost to my understanding, they habitually chose people of lower class and quality than themselves to be their rulers. Jimmy Carter, the one president who saw this bitter truth that American citizens' morals were higher than their government's morals and uttered the heresy in public, time after time, was tossed out of office after a single term. Some truths about rulers were unwelcome in the great republic.

Two presidents, Kennedy and Clinton, had great difficulty in getting their minds to work above the level of the bellybutton. Kennedy, son of a bootlegger and Nazi sympathizer who bought the office for him, insisted on bedding strange women in the White House, including Mafia dolls who may have had something to do with his eventual assassination. Another president, Reagan, took office in the early stages of Alzheimer's disease and had difficulty focussing his mind on anything, except to make the rich richer and the poor poorer, which he succeeded in doing by tax measures.

All three men were popular, as the American press measures popularity, but in fact not one of them was. They were in office by default. If the people who declined to take part in the democratic process had re-entered political life there is no way we can imagine who might have led America, but it would have been none of the above. You would never have known it by watching TV or reading newspapers, but by the year 2000 most Americans no longer cared.

If they did not object to what the press fed them, it was out of a respect for enthusiasm and salesmanship. Generous, fair-minded and optimistic as he may be, the American has a fault that is as curious as it is unnecessary. He has to boast. Bullshitting is the vulgar term in our age; doubtless you people down the timeline have a similar one. Americans were born with the impulse to bullshit foreigners and if no foreigners were at hand, they would bullshit one another. Thus the average American could not only tell himself but could also believe that his country had never lost a war, as if 1812 and Vietnam had never happened. He believed with a genuine passion that the US constitution, written in 1778, was a true and perfect blueprint for good government, in spite of it having to be amended twenty-seven times by the year 2000.

All this had its effects on Canada. Our numbers were almost always a tenth of the Americans, except in the days of New France, when we were a meagre two and a half percent of their population. This probably still holds true in your time unless climate change has altered our relative strengths or free trade has wiped out almost all the boundary between the countries.

Being so heavily influenced by American bullshit, Canadians also accepted all sorts of outrageously wrong words and pasted the meanings on them that suited the chattering classes of their day. Democracy was such a word, sacred, like motherhood, and, by 2000, overtaking and passing motherhood in the goodness sweepstakes race because motherhood had begun to become a sign of sinister self-interest.

Of course, we did not have democracy. No nation ever did, although the Greeks of Athens, some small towns in New England, the Icelanders and some North American Native Indian tribes came close for a while, later rearranging their systems to suit the real world.

True democracy was, in any case, an outrageous notion. How can any decent man support the proposition that 15 million Canadians have the unchallenged right to butcher, barbecue and eat the other 14,999,999? Not only the common people but also the intellectuals always knew better, although usually they found it prudent not to make their views public. A few did.

Baron de Tocqueville of France, examining the recently founded United States of America, perceived the threat of what he called the tyranny of the majority. He pointed out that when Americans of that day complained of tyrannies abroad, such as the French kings, they failed to realize the tyrant king left his subjects alone for the most part. He grabbed taxes from them, too many in the end, but for the most part he kept out of their lives. The new democratic government of the United States of America might, said Tocqueville, intrude into every aspect of the citizen's life. That is exactly what has happened.

You may well ask why did we tolerate so barbarous an idea as half the people killing the other half for a picnic? The answer is that we knew in our hearts that it wasn't real. The word *democracy* was Goodspeak. Everybody knew that. So the most successful political leaders invoked it on every occasion, as the Mexican invokes the Virgin of Guadalupe. However, for the good of all, the democracy notion is not allowed to interfere unduly with daily life.

As the twentieth century plodded out, science in its fullest glory, human relationships moribund, the people either turned away from governing themselves or, if they were disciples of Trotsky, turned to street demonstrations such as hadn't been seen since the storming of the Bastille. Like the storming of the Bastille, which rescued nobody except a few of the despised aristocrats, these protests were for the most part futile, just sound and light displays, masses of middle-class youngsters with too little to do with their time shouting "Do it my way or I'll hold my breath and turn blue!" They were able to disrupt ordinary affairs, occasionally with much property damage and danger to innocent lives, because of the tolerance and general wimpish disinterest of the society they sought to overthrow. Napoleon knew the answer: a whiff of grapeshot. In the year 2000 he would have been investigated, charged, tried by kangaroo court and disgraced, over a period of ten years or so, for using pepper spray or German shepherd dogs who barked. From Gandhi on, civil disobedience has depended for success upon the extreme civility of rulers. Ours of today tolerate it less through good manners and more through an innate disinterest in the democratic representative process.

A more effective form of protest than smearing yourself with your own shit, so the riot squad don't like handling you, is lobbying. These are the professional persuaders who crowd the courts of our rulers, seeking special treatment for those they represent. Lobbyists also approach elected people, but in recent years their efforts are spent increasingly on the elected people's functionaries. In the 1960s one of Ottawa's most famed and successful lobbyists had a simple rule for all who worked in his organization: "Never cross Wellington Street." Translation: Never deal with the elected people on Parliament Hill; deal with the mandarins in the bureaucratic castles of lower town.

One more new force was introduced in the second half of that century. Voting blocs appeared. Blocs of votes were delivered for or against parties on such issues as abortion laws, pesticide use or the right to offer public prayers at football games. We had, by 2000, government by pressure groups and Parliament was just one more pressure group, often not the dominant one. What had happened was that we had adopted fascism, but that word needs explanation, now and probably in future.

Fascism was developed in Italy in the 1920s. Germany adopted a form of it in the '30s, as did Oswald Mosley in England and other political experimentalists. It was, as presented in those years, a totalitarian, repressive system of government. The Russians, who also adopted totalitarianism and repression, chose to call their system communism, but there was little difference between the two for those who went to the wall before the firing squads.

There was, in the realm of fancy, such a thing as pure fascism and it had a logic. The pure fascist rejected democracy because too many ignorant people were voting for things they did not understand and doing so with too much hope and enthusiasm. Fascism foresaw a state operated by power groups. Every section of society would have its share of governance. This system, never achieved—no system ever is—envisaged rule somewhat like that of the medieval trade guilds, closed societies with public faces. In fascism every societal group—doctors, lawyers, tree planters, ditch diggers, poets, college professors and prostitutes—would have representatives in government who spoke for their interests. I have never been able to warm to the theory, because I don't believe that the ditch diggers will ever be as successful as the lawyers or the industrialists in promoting their cause, but my opinion is not a part of this chapter.

Unfortunately the word *fascist* has been rendered almost useless since the Second World War. The Stalinist Communists, who so much resembled the fascists in their brutality and cruelty, chose the word to mean People's Enemy. Trotsky was dead by then, murdered by Stalin's command, and a new demon had to be created.

For less sensible reasons, most of the western world accepted this communist hagiography, and by the 1990s most of us were applying the word *fascist* to anybody who disagreed with us about anything. If you didn't like parsnips and somebody else did, they looked a bit fascist to you. Racists were fascists and so were the promoters of professional rodeo and people who were insufficiently fond of whales. Words sometimes prevent us from learning the most valuable meanings of history.

I recall a neighbour who was a sculptor, a malcontent of the old tradition, bohemian, bearded, who ostentatiously ground his own coffee. He talked at tiresome length of his political vision that artists, geographers, priests, dentists and deep-sea pile drivers should each have their own representation in governing the state. I never had the heart to tell him that he was fascist. He was convinced he was a pure socialist and he fought hard for that party each election.

To work well, fascism (the real kind) required an authoritarian and powerful state. It might or might not be unkind but it was stern, a disciplinarian father who rewarded goodness and punished badness, always by his definitions of those words. Its rules and regulations were beyond numbering. Freedom, as Benito Mussolini put it, was something for cavemen. Civilized people were expected to grow out of it as, indeed, seems to have happened to a considerable degree.

The amazing thing is that we fought a terrible war against Fascism and associated Nazism and, later, Communism, all in the name of freedom. Now, more than half a century after we beat them, we have adopted most of their policies.

With one honourable exception, racism, we pursue pretty much the same policies as Hitler's Germany, Mussolini's Italy and the horrid futurism of *1984* and *Brave New World*.

In this country we now have the Thought Police, who can persecute us not for what we do or say but for what they believe we might think. With disapproval of only one-third of the public, we kill the unwanted among us by sanitized procedures. Almost one-fifth of the babies conceived are aborted. Yet majority decisions aren't always good ones, as the Germans were later to agree after electing Hitler in a fair and democratic election by 90 percent of the votes. We now have Star Chamber Courts in which the same people are policemen, prosecutors and judges who, together, invent both the crime and the punishment. As our Supreme Court of Canada has confirmed, some Canadian citizens are more equal than others before the law. It may be said that these perversions are not a part of fascist philosophy but an aberration and that I, too, am guilty of using the word as a catch-all epithet. However, all these things are too closely linked to the operational fascism we fought against to be passed over.

Who turned us fascist?

For the most part, the changes have been brought about by governments that abhor the very word and will go to any length to find substitute words, such as welfare state. Most of the fascism introduced into our lives is an attempt to produce good behaviour by laws and regulations, and when it fails, as we fallible humans so often make it fail, the solution must be even more laws and even more regulations. To failed laws, we add new ones that also fail. Again, the fascist spirit, the loving but stern father who knows what is best for us. Sooner or later, it is reasoned, we will learn and turkeys will enjoy Thanksgiving just as much as we do.

The strength of the lobbyists and the power groups is now so apparent that none dispute it and the press is more likely to turn to the president of some Whippet, Wild Bird and Croquet Society than to a Member of Parliament to judge what new direction our society should take.

What is so troubling is that in the true fascist state, the very strong become stronger and the weak are left making noises that nobody hears. Mothers Against Drunk Driving, an admirable group, are never going to replace the United Auto Workers or the mining industry as a force in this land.

John Ralston Saul, one of our country's most able thinkers, calls our society corporatist and lists its many faults under that name. He despaired, I suppose, of using the word *fascist* because it is so rarely understood. The grievous faults he calls corporatism are fascism.

Today's fascism has torn families apart, stolen from the poor to give to the rich and committed unspeakable cruelties upon people guilty of no worse offence than being different. However, fascism is an idea whose time has come and it must run its course until it fades, as all ideas do. One party may replace another in the

House of Commons but fascism will grow and prosper as a philosophy with little let or hindrance.

In the end fascism will fail, if only because all systems do. Even now there is a general recognition that although all the trades and professions of the land may join to form an unbreakable bundle of sticks—the symbol bequeathed us by the Romans, who were a notorious bunch of sons of bitches—it is disturbingly noticeable that the strongest sticks do not do most of the supporting.

I hope that by the time you read this, dear descendant, fascism will have failed. It probably will continue to thrive and grow for as long as I live.

Pretend You Paid For This Advice

ADVICE, THEY SAY, IS WORTH WHAT YOU PAY FOR IT. Lawyers are particularly fond of that adage, and they are smart people. So, if it is to do you any good, pretend you paid good money for this advice. Of course, I must confess I can offer no good advice to the descendants two or three generations away, whose world I cannot know. However, there will be people of my own time reading this and to them I owe a few words of practical advice.

First, as the millennium begins, know your enemy, which is no longer wind, weather, crop failure, plague or war but may be your government. All governments are now more tyrannical than a few decades ago, and although their goals are almost always benign, they have built an apparatus of state control that could easily be seized and operated for the opposite purpose. Beware Big Brother, he is very near and very strong. However, avoid despair. The very size of the state apparatus for surveillance and control of the citizens operates in your favour.

The original Big Brother of George Orwell's imagination never attempted to control the entire population. His surveillance was of only a small number of elite, the members of his party. The mass of the population were kept quiet with bread and circuses. No secret police interfered in their lives, meagre though those lives were. Not only Soviet Russia but also the western nations— Canada, the United States and the countries of Western and Eastern Europe—attempted something awesomely larger. They would record all the movements, words and attitudes of all the citizens. They achieved a lot in this dire pursuit. In the year 2000 I demanded the federal government tell me how much data it had collected on me. It sent me a partial list. I wearied of reading it soon and even stopped counting the items at 1,500. They had obtained a lot of detail, every bit of it without my permission being asked or given.

Those who have retained any taste for freedom and privacy, mostly people in their seventies who can remember the freer nation we once were, must be depressed by measuring how far the modern state has advanced toward total surveillance—Soviet Russia first, the rest of us now scrambling to catch up to her dismal record. How far the Soviets advanced toward controlling everybody can be studied best by reading the exhaustive examination of the Soviets in Brezhnev's time by Hedrick Smith of the *New York Times* in his book *The Russians*. He describes the constant, pervasive fear of being seen or heard behaving with political incorrectness. Yet curiously enough, Smith found there was much hope for the ordinary citizen in that land which had the highest ratio of police officers to citizens in human history. He describes in detail how, during the 1970s, the Russian people learned to distinguish between dangerous political crimes that could send one to Siberia and the ordinary crimes such as burglary and theft that, in the press of events, might be overlooked entirely.

Russian citizens sought and obtained some freedom amid what was supposed to be total tyranny, but by methods which make one despair to read of them. The main lesson to be learned: the Russian people knew their enemy, the Soviet state, and although Mr. Smith could not be expected to foresee it, that enemy was eventually vanquished, thanks to the courage of a few men such as Nikita Khrushchev and Mikhail Gorbachev and the massive, cleverly concealed determination of individual men and women to seize freedom when it was offered. In Smith's years in the Soviet Union, people recognized that their state apparatus was where almost all power lay and, being servants of the state, they protected themselves at state expense by skilful malingering. "If they will continue to pretend to pay us, we will continue to pretend that we are working." The people also found gaps in their prison walls, memorized the locations and learned to pass easily through them to pursue their own goals, often but not always by criminal activities.

Any people at any time learn where the eagle sits. In the late '60s and early '70s, New York police had lost control of their streets and ordinary citizens were afraid to be outdoors. At that period the Canadian government used to issue printed warnings to the MPs of our UN delegation that read like an instruction sheet for Sarajevo people during the ethnic cleansing period. "Do not leave a taxi unless it can deliver you directly opposite the door of your restaurant. Go directly inside, quickly." We had difficulty recruiting MPs to fill our UN delegation in New York.

Yet in that dangerous period there was an old lady who wandered those streets with hundreds of thousands of dollars inside a shabby shopping bag. She was a courier for the narcotics traders. All criminals knew it. She was as safe as in God's vest pocket because she came from where the eagle sat.

Here in the state of Sinaloa, in Mexico, the drug gangs routinely execute government and court officials and recently, on the nearby north-south main Mexican highway, at least one bus a week is pulled over by men with AK-47s—they call them the goathorn guns because of the shape of the magazine—who take all the money and jewellery from the passengers. We are not sure what the position of the police is in this, particularly since one of them was also executed on the highway, but we know that the eagle does not sit in the state capital of Sinaloa.

Find where the power lies in your region and learn to use it or, if it be one that violates your principles, how to avoid it; the important thing is to know it.

Much more important to the protection of common people, not only the detection but also the punishment of crime must be arranged by bureaucrats, who, in the usual way, are chiefly interested in the three Ps—pay, pension, perks—with carrying out their duties ranking number four on the list of things they must do. The bureaucrats are not bad, cruel or wicked people; they are people caught up in the ritual dances at the rulers' courts. Most entered the public service with the intention of providing exactly that, service, but have ended up as time servers, frustrated by the curtain of deadwood they usually find at the top of their department and the mindless devotion to paper that clogs the arteries of all bureaucracies. A general cynicism overwhelms most of them.

Only those who have seen them in action at first hand can appreciate their inefficiency. When I was a British Columbia police commissioner, we used to hold regular meetings to deal with the problem of how to get complaints against police officers transferred to departmental investigators while the case was fresh. Some letters of complaint, rerouted from the attorney general's office, took a month, and more, to be sent to our Vancouver office, which was a half day distant by courier, five minutes by fax machine, two minutes by e-mail. When I told the attorney general about this delay, which seemed to me, new on the job, incredible, he gave a despairing giggle. "It takes up to four days for mail to get from the front door to me, and the front door is only twenty steps away."

In Mexico a police commissioner could have solved this problem by paying a Victoria secretary or mail clerk a five dollar bribe (called *la mordida*, "the little nibble") for every complaint she forwarded by fax or e-mail. At year's end, she might have had enough to buy a new dress, no more, but immense good would have been accomplished—all the investigations would have been better and speedier.

Instead we wasted thousands of dollars because the loftier regions of the service insisted we meet and study flow charts about this, under leadership of a civil servant who boasted that in his briefcase he had letters needing attention that had lain there for weeks. "Not even my secretary knows about these cases."

I held about the lowest rank of the five or six people who would attend these meetings, that of assistant deputy minister, pay scale then in the $60,000 to $70,000 range, in 1970 dollars.

The total cost of our wasted hours in these meetings must have been monstrous. It would have bought dresses or neckties for every civil servant in Victoria. Yet we accomplished nothing. Three years later, when I resigned, declaring that I was wasting my time and the public's money (no newspaper found the remark worthy of comment), the problem of getting mail from Victoria to Vancouver was still unsolved and may well be to this day.

To see people like these as a mighty conspiracy that will sniff out every crime we commit and punish us for it is completely unrealistic.

In a strange reversal of the rulers' intentions, the ordinary people are in many ways protected against prosecution by the sheer weight of modern law. There have long been far too many laws for even the most devoted practitioners of the police state to expect to see them implemented. The courts would collapse under the weight of accumulated cases to be heard.

The rulers themselves recognized this and by century's end only a few crimes were dealt with as crimes. Even thirty years before, when the number of federal laws and regulations having the force of law was only about 17,000, probably half or a third of today's number, we had already reached the point where scarcely any citizen could go from daybreak to dark without breaking laws, most of which he wouldn't know if they ran up and bit him on the ass.

The Law Reform Commission of Canada, in a report from the early '70s (it began with Seneca's dictum: "The more the laws, the more the criminals"), stated then that the act of breaking a law and being caught was no longer viewed by the rulers as sufficient reason for trial and punishment. Whether or not prosecution resulted when a criminal was identified was largely a bureaucratic decision to proceed or not proceed with prosecution. In the ocean of law in which we now paddle, trying to keep our heads above water, a few illegal gulps are inevitable, expected and largely ignored. You can safely break most minor laws.

This has, of course, made the public contemptuous of almost all law, but that never seems to bother the rulers. Perhaps it is because they live too far from the real world. Their insulation from the people, brought about by sycophancy and by various forms of censorship, is best described in this passage: "The government hears only its own voice while all the time deceiving itself, affecting to hear the voices of the people while demanding that they also support the pretence. And on their side, the people either partly succumb to political skepticism or completely turn away from public life and become a crowd of individuals, each living for his own private existence." The author was Karl Marx, a man who, like Adam Smith and other economic observers, is quoted most often and most approvingly by people who have never read him and use his words to promote policies alien to his ideas. Marx's creed, distorted, led to the most complete censorship of print ever known in the world in the Soviet Union, a system almost exactly like that of the Ministry of Truth in Orwell's *1984*, an organization devoted to lying.

Given this separation between rulers and ruled, in which we seem anxious to catch up to the Soviets and other tyrannies at the close of the twentieth century, terrible things could happen. In northern British Columbia the Goods and Services Tax people, who unlike private companies are under no obligation to prove in court that they have a right to snatch somebody's money, seized an elderly man's total assets and auctioned them off to pay a GST bill. Later, it turned out he had no GST bill. He didn't owe them a cent. They gave him back the pittance they received when auctioning his property. Distress auction sales seldom bring true value bids. He could have sued for the true value of those goods once it was discovered they had been wrongly seized, except for one thing: he couldn't. In the new fascist state, scarcely any private citizen can get into the Supreme Court of Canada without the backing of some large corporation, a union, a society or someone with very deep pockets. The court is designed to serve institutions, not deal in the outdated notion of the free citizen who is so captious as to consider himself as good as his government.

A difficulty in confronting bureaucratic errors or intransigence is that when you reveal that the error is not yours but theirs, you arouse an enmity that may become bitter. Such a case wound up in the federal court in British Columbia. An old army vet, retired on pension, had a house, a wife, a pet dog and a boat big enough to sleep aboard and planned to enjoy them all in his last years. Except for the wife, he lost them all to Canada Customs.

Somebody reported he was using his boat to smuggle something illegal—booze, drugs or cigarettes—into Canada. Since he had been in the Provost Corps it is not hard to judge who slipped the false information to Customs (policemen are seldom popular figures), but the result was horrendous. Failing to discover the slightest evidence, the Customs people went berserk, seized the boat, which eventually sank at its moorings, and subjected the old man to merciless and continuous investigation. The less they discovered, the greater their anger.

The federal judge who heard this case found for the old man and damned the Canada Customs agents and their top management in terms so scathing as to be seldom heard in a court of law. He found the behaviour had been so outrageous and sometimes illegal that in addition to ordering restitution he imposed heavy punitive damages. However, nobody in the department was ever fired, demoted or reprimanded. There had been plenty of time for cover-ass and it turned out that, in spite of what the judge had said, nobody was to blame for anything. Of two men named specifically by the judge, one retired to private business and the other won promotion in the department. Taxpayers like me paid the quarter of a million dollars awarded and, diminished as they were by lawyers' fees, they came too late to be much help to the old chap anyway.

Moral: never be 100 percent right when a ruler's representative is trying to win brownie points by proving you wrong.

I can remember biting my tongue until it bled in the face of such bureaucratic arrogance. My wife and I, seized by one of the better impulses of a lifetime and determined to proceed in a venture that we were assured could never succeed, adopted a little Mexican girl who remains, a young married woman, one of four children who brighten my life today. Early in the proceedings we required a US visa so we could take her to Seattle on a one-day trip to obtain papers at the Canadian consulate there.

An American immigration official at the United States Consulate in Vancouver found our request irregular and assured us he had no intention of permitting any such thing for, like a true bureaucrat, he detested irregularity. He lectured me about Canadian laxness in policing our borders. It was no time and certainly not an occasion to point out that his own country had permitted 15 to 20 percent of the entire population of Mexico to enter the US illegally. I meekly, quietly offered him papers I had brought to the consulate. They were my bank accounts, a statement from the Royal Canadian Mounted Police that I had no criminal record and a character reference from a judge. He tossed them back at me unread. "We find papers like these tend to be self-serving," he said. I couldn't dispute that judgment but I wondered if he could hear what he was saying.

Finally he said we could come back and try again. "But I would want to see a great deal of documentation."

"What documents would you want?" I asked.

I will never forget him, that little pinstriped New York nit. He fixed a cold eye on me and said, "I am not going to tell YOU!"

We went back a few days later, encountered a sensible young woman who asked a few sensible questions, and were sent on our way with our needed visa in a few minutes. If I had kicked the earlier idiot in the ass I might have improved him but we would never have got the paper we needed.

We were lucky. Others are not.

There is the case in which the Canada Customs and Revenue Agency garnisheed almost all a Prairie family's income to pay income tax arrears. The department is supposed to be forbidden by law to leave a family without food and shelter in garnishee actions but that law was ignored, as so many laws are by our rulers. The wife and mother finally took out a broad-based life insurance policy on herself that did not exclude suicide, then killed herself so the insurance payment could satisfy Revenue Canada and rescue her hungry children.

I wrote commenting bitterly on such cases to an Ottawa friend, a veteran of the House who happens to be one of the finest men I ever knew. He was hard-working, honest, forthright, decisive, kind and just plain decent. I have known few men I admire more. Yet when I once deplored the power of unelected civil servants to visit misery on people, he replied, almost casually, "Yes, things go wrong. But we can always correct the situation."

It can't always be rectified. Nothing can restore that old man's retirement savings. Nothing can bring that woman back to her family.

I mention my friend for the very reason that he is a fine man, and I continue to admire him tremendously. Yet life in the nation's capital had induced in him a strangely indifferent frame of mind, that he could speak so casually of situations that he and the other MPs had helped create but which had not wreaked their havoc upon them or their families. Although the circumstances were different, that Prairie wife and mother is every bit as dead as the peasant whom a nobleman of pre-revolutionary France shot and killed just for the sport of it and because he could get away with it.

For government, the knowledge of what really happens in Canada diminishes by the square of the distance from Parliament Hill. The people beyond the Ottawa Valley lose their humanity and become statistics. All government invites that attitude.

The situation has of course been made far worse by the new system of electing MPs to serve a party first and the voters at home second, if at all.

One cannot help but wonder how Canada reached this condition. Unless you believe it is a monstrous conspiracy by the rulers, which I do not, then the reason has to lie with the people themselves. In the long run, people get the kind of government they deserve in any country. Individually and then in groups, we have allowed ourselves to believe that laws and regulations can solve all man's ailments and once we have enough of them on the statute books we shall enter a golden age.

This impulse to regimentation is not unusual in Europe. Hitler's and Stalin's people did no more than extend the state controls already at hand. Even in 2002, when the totalitarian regimes were supposedly defeated, we can be astounded by the degree of state control on the continent, with Britain recently joining in building new and bigger termite hills. I recall a Canadian municipal police chief who attended a conference on prison reform in the Netherlands. He noted such state controls as the issuance of internal passports so citizens could move around, also that one needed government permission to move to a different town or city. He told his hosts, "I am not impressed with the fact that you have so many prisoners out on the streets on ticket-of-leave arrangements. Your entire country is a prison."

Yet with those words this man raised a large unanswered question about his own country. Most of the Canadian people are of European origin and most of them left Europe to find freedom on this continent. My first ancestor on the male side came here in 1640 and today more than 30,000 of his descendants are scattered around North America. I have never heard of even one of them who wanted to move back to Europe. Yet, having broken off Europe's shackles and come across the ocean in search of freedom, we are now extinguishing freedom at a rate rivalling the tired, anal retentive old nations of the continent. Why? Nobody knows. Worse, nobody is asking.

I return to the subject of advice. If one cannot advise the people unborn, what advice can be offered those alive today who read this book?

First, study your rulers, learn their strengths and their weaknesses and quietly, privately, carve out for yourself a haven where you can live decently, behave honourably and breathe fresh air. Unless you are going into the political arena to attempt to make changes, in which case may Almighty God and millions of dollars be with you, keep a low profile. Make it your goal to not be noticed by people in power.

As I have suggested, you may confuse those people fairly easily. A friend who is both an American and a Canadian citizen keeps two sets of passports, driver's licences, tax receipts and Lions club memberships to clearly identify him as being of one or the other nationality. He moves his wallets from one pocket to the other and shifts car licence plates as needed, depending on which identity he finds convenient to adopt at the moment. Both identities are legal.

There is much more that you can do to confuse your rulers. The details are readily available in such publications as those of Eden Press, which offer abundant information on hiding your money and yourself from public records. Then there are small things, easily done. By paying cash for everything you can wipe out much of the paper trail you leave each day in your normal life. Some institutions may refuse to accept cash instead of credit cards, bank cards or cheques but remember they have no legal right to do so. Cash is still a legitimate method of payment. You could enforce your right to pay cash through the courts, although it would scarcely be worthwhile in this case, because avoiding public appearances is your object, not making them. So give them plastic when they insist. There aren't many who will insist, and people in the underground economy, with whom everybody has dealings from time to time, welcome old-fashioned money.

I have difficulty talking about the underground economy. All of us indulge in it occasionally in small ways but many Canadians have gone completely underground. Estimates run from a low of 10 percent to a high of 20. Morally you may feel justified in going underground, considering that the rulers can now seize money they find in your possession and refuse to give it back until you prove that you came by it honestly. If you do not have explanations they consider acceptable, they keep the money. Like just about every act of tyranny ever undertaken, this is done for our own good. This law hit narcotics traffickers. Nobody mentions that they were made rich by the state's grand experiment in prohibition of some of the narcotic drugs. Neither, of course, does anyone ask aloud what business it is of any government if a citizen chooses to damage his brains and his physical health by taking narcotics, something that became an offence only at the beginning of the last century. In years to come, my descendants may look back on the money seizure legislation as marking a period of human history when private property rights ceased to be respected and as a substitute the state (of "eminent domain," to use the legal term) undertook to decide the amount of money, property or land to which we might claim some degree of possession. So some may say that today's citizen, being relieved of all true ownership of his property, is also relieved of all true duty to share any of it with his rulers and that underground is the only way to go.

This, however, is not human nature. We are individuals, striving to be free, but we are also social animals. We do many things collectively by choices both conscious and unconscious. In the very marrow of our bones is an urge to protect the weak, to rescue the imperilled, to love our fellow man. All people have a great sense of fairness. On the day this page was written the *New York Times* reports from the journal *Nature* that scientists feel they have proven that there is a basic human predilection to punish those who cheat on the social contract. "Human beings are elaborately, ineluctably social creatures... [there is] such a readiness to trust others, to behave civilly in a crowd, to play the occasional good Samaritan—all behaviors that we laud and endorse could not have developed without a corresponding readiness to catch and to punish the Cheat." We will at our own cost, altruistically, punish cheats, even where our kin are not involved.

The underground economy is a form of cheating and as you become increasingly aware of this, your nature will be at war with yourself. You will sense that if the 10 or 20 percent of underground people increases to 40 or 50 percent, the country will grind to a halt, as happened in this year of 2002 in Argentina.

Every man must reach his own accommodation, never forgetting how much it is worth to sleep soundly at night without fearing the midnight knock on the door.

An even more ominous development, at time of writing, is that the institution of the family is fading rapidly. In my lifetime we began with the three-generation household, with the children learning about how life begins with their mother having a new baby and knowing about the end of life through Grandmother and Grandfather dying in the same upstairs bedroom. Next came the two-generation household of parents and children. Now we have the single parent household, in which less than half the children being born will reach age 18 with the same pair of adults with which they began. I think this is an unfortunate development. So does the American philosopher Francis Fukuyama, one of the most brilliant of our futurists, who expects that even in his family's original homeland, Japan, the family institution will fade away. He doesn't like it but attempts to write about what he sees as truth, welcome or unwelcome. So do I.

Something must reinforce or replace the family unit. I cannot see what, but it must be there for us to use and somehow we will find it—our universe has a way of providing us with the essentials.

Man cannot travel alone from birth to death, he not only craves, he also needs, must have, a source of support that is rendered without question and without restraint, without any pause to judge whether or not he merits it, a love that is simply there, a well of pure, clear water that does not run dry. Perhaps some replacement of the family can be found in another of life's greatest blessings, friendship.

A replacement for the safe and secure refuge of family will emerge. So will a glorious flowering of the arts and a limitless bull market on Wall Street. But this is like predicting rain in the Sahara, it is a safe thing to do. You know you will be proven right, providing you don't attach a time to your forecast. Predicting when these things will happen is the whole trick of it. If I knew the when of any of these matters I would rule the entire world. Without the dimension of time factored tightly into a prediction the words are no more than chewed air and I shall waste no more space on prognostication here.

At the end of the day you will find that what mattered was not the money or honours you obtained or the pleasures you experienced; what is most precious is the friendships you made. One of the reasons that many old people appear to lose interest in living and quickly fade away to the grave is that so many of their friends have already gone and they feel they might as well follow because they are lonely.

So be brave. You are far more powerful than you realize. The rulers move and coax us one way or another but no matter how many regiments of law and regulations they raise, they seldom defeat the guerrilla citizen.

If you want proof of this, take the next forecast by the world's best experts of a recession, a bull market or a landslide election victory by somebody. They are rarely correct. Why? Because they use their own large logic while individuals in their multitudes use their own small logics and arrive at the conclusions that matter. The ultimate movement in society is decided by a multitude of small decisions, made privately, for private reasons. In the face of this instinctive logical thought of the private citizens, all the powers of the great wither. Remember the answer to the question of who really runs Canada, asked in the chapter on conspiracy. Nobody runs Canada.

Wisdoms Gone Old and Stale

BEWARE THE RIGHTEOUS MAN

INTELLECTUALS COME AND GO, the just, the unjust and the castrated. As suggested elsewhere they may do either good or harm, like rain or stumping powder. The righteous man is another matter, and I am grateful forever to my father for one of the few pieces of advice he ever offered me. Beware the righteous man, for the fires of hell burn in him.

Most of the evils in this world are the work of righteous men. Evil, pray remember, is a thing far worse than wrongs. Most of us commit wrongs from time to time, often by nothing more than mere thoughtlessness or carelessness. Evil is different. It is darker, crueller and more damaging than mere wrongdoing. The righteous, too pure to need salvation, are prone to evil more often than to thoughtlessness.

The worst of crimes and cruelties are the field of the righteous. Again, like the intellectuals listed in the chapter on that subject, Torquemada, Heinrich Himmler and a host of other historic figures dripping in the blood of innocents were men suffused with their own sense of righteousness.

They should not be mistaken for psychopaths, who also commit much evil in the world. Unlike the righteous, the psychopath knows very well the difference between right and wrong but he polishes his considerable skill as an actor to imitate those who do right. His righteousness is calculated and skilfully organized, and he can slice up an innocent man with no more sense of feeling than he would apply to cutting open a cabbage. It is a grievous flaw that is believed to originate in the brain mechanism. Most children are said to go through a partially psychopathic period in adolescence and the problem appears to lessen with age. Psychopaths who reach their sixties are pretty much like the rest of us.

Not the righteous man. He is sublimely unconscious that there can be anything wrong with his behaviour. He seeks no disguises; he is proud of what he is. Most of the righteous, like most of the slightly psychopathic, go through life doing no harm beyond trying the patience of those around them. Sometimes they are catastrophes.

Decent people—do I use that word too often? If so, too bad, it is the correct word—do not classify themselves as righteous. They have too much natural humility, too much common sense and too ready a sense of humour. Fanatics, on the other hand, are almost always righteous.

A criminal lawyer of my acquaintance identified these people crisply, as lawyers often can. "There is no witness so hard to cross-examine as the righteous man. He is serene, he is calm, he is confident and he often impresses even the smartest jurymen immensely. You may know that he lies through his teeth in testifying. He may or may not know it himself, but it doesn't matter to him. Even if he lies he knows he is a superior being in quest of the greater good for men lesser than himself. He is damn near unshakeable."

Knowing that the end justifies the means and that he, with some co-operation by the Almighty, is the one to know what that proper end should be, the righteous man speaks and acts accordingly, without reference to either state-made or moral laws. He is above the law. His favourite author is the old Spanish monk Baltasar Gracián, who wrote a book that should have landed him in the Inquisition's prisons but did not because, as he put it, "To the just, no laws, to the wise, no counsel." Gracián was a righteous man.

The righteous experience great difficulty in distinguishing right from wrong. Some just can't do it at all. No matter what they have done, a sense of guilt never much disturbs their serene passage through life. Nothing is to be gained by close identification, but I can recall more than one politician who was found with money he should not have had doing things with it that he should not have done. Some are tried in criminal courts and some just resign in disgrace for unethical behaviour. Both before and after those sorry events, they remain buoyant, cheerful and, to many, convincingly correct. They know their own righteousness. How could contrary opinions, even the opinions of judges and juries, be of any matter? They live long and die secure in that belief. If it turns out that the story about purgatory is true, they will never understand how they could have ended up in such a place; some error has been made and will soon be corrected.

The most dangerous form of righteousness is called Messianism. The messianic man has found pure truth, pure justice, pure honour, and God is his associate. Sometimes God is his only associate; all the rest are sullied and sinful.

Beware the righteous man but do not fear to resist him and do it early, when he first attempts to dazzle you with the light of his blazing purity. Take courage from the Christian Bible. It's a book I like to quote from time to time, to lend a tone of elegance and scholarship that some find lacking in my style of writing. So be bold. Prov. 28:1: "The wicked flea, when no man pursueth but the righteous, is bold as a lion." Did I get that wrong?

THE SEVEN SINS AREN'T SO DEADLY

He has all of the virtues I dislike and none of the vices I admire.
— Winston Churchill on Stafford Cripps

AT THE END OF THE DAY, there are few truisms that don't cry out for re-examination as to truth. The seven deadly sins, promulgated by the medieval church, will do for a sample.

The church did not specify acts, such as murder, arson and rape, as sins because those are crimes. That was eminently sensible. Sins, which may include the commission of many crimes, are matters of the soul, not of man-made law, and it was the quality of the soul that the seven deadly sins addressed. Poorly, however.

What were those seven deadly sins? The list: lust, gluttony, avarice, sloth, anger, envy and pride.

With the sole exception of envy, a mean and corrosive sentiment, there isn't one of the above I have not thoroughly enjoyed on many occasions. Lust, gluttony, sloth? Who doesn't want some of that in their life? Even anger can claim pride of place on some occasions. When my old friend Doug Hogarth, a judge, was being buried, a secretary said at his funeral, "He got angry sometimes, but he always got angry about the right things."

There were also seven contrary virtues, and for some reason several of these have a tiresome, whining quality to them. The list: humility, kindness, abstinence, chastity, patience, liberality and diligence.

Kindness is the only one I warm to, plus perhaps liberality, if only for the reason that the lunatic right in the United States reacts to that word the way vampires react to crosses and garlic cloves. Humility? The people's humility kept churchmen and other rogues in power for centuries. Humility is a Croatian peasant who, when a priest passed, was expected to kneel and cross himself. Abstinence? The word reminds me of the women I failed to take to bed when they wanted me to. Patience and diligence are admirable in most people but in some they become a plain pain in the ass. Chastity? Spare us.

One of the good things that had happened in our society by the year 2002 was that there wasn't one person in a thousand who could list the seven deadly sins and not one in 100,000 who thought they were worth knowing.

The seven deadly sins and virtues are part of the rubbish in our basement that we don't get around to throwing out. Or, on second thoughts, perhaps we have; if so, good.

THE TRUTH ABOUT LYING

THERE ARE STILL PEOPLE AROUND who say that the lie which looks like the truth is the worst kind of a lie. Why do they keep talking this way? A lie that looks like the truth is the very best kind of a lie—it is the least likely to be discovered, the most likely to achieve its purpose.

The only people for whom the lie that looks like the truth is not the best kind of lie are those such as Mark Twain, Stephen Leacock, P.J. O'Rourke and other humourists who delight us with stories so absurd that nobody could ever mistake them for truth. Most of us know at least three or four good liar types. There is the one who wants to amuse us with wild flights of imagination and wit. Another can share any ordinary experience with us and then at a later date embellish the truth about our doings so extravagantly that we can scarcely recognize either ourselves or the events. He brightens otherwise dull days. Also, roguery often becomes more entertaining, even if not acceptable, with lies. My grandfather, a man of Puritan bent for almost all his life, told with pleasure about the poacher he caught waiting in the bushes beside his net in my grandfather's salmon river. "Ah sir, I see we are here on the same errand. I was just waiting for him to come and pull that net." Also there is the compulsive liar who can't seem to control himself, the man who, when he could safely stand flat-footed on the ground and tell you the truth, will climb a tree so he can tell you a lie.

Yet the word *liar* is one of the least pleasant in our language. Our courts and our parliaments seek to identify and punish those who are not truthful. The man who escapes his just desserts by lying seems to attract a special scorn from most people, including one whom I would not need a long stick to touch. Like a great many people, I still find myself taking the wrong, illogical side of the German officer story. Apocryphal as it probably is, this is a story of Americans interrogating a senior German officer in 1915 on suspicion of spying. He was in the United States ostensibly as a civilian member of a trade delegation. An interrogator finally asked him, "Will you, on your word of honour as a German officer, assure us that you were not spying?" He wouldn't do it.

Anybody can say that if the Americans didn't then shoot him, his own people should have when he returned to Germany. He had betrayed his trust and his country for reasons of pure personal pride. Such is the irrefutable logic of the German officer story but I admire the man, and because I do the whole matter of truth and falsehood becomes distorted and confused.

We are, after all, almost all taught to lie at our mother's knee. "Tell Auntie Maude how you enjoyed *Bible Stories of All Nations*."

"I didn't enjoy it, I hated it."

"Tell her you liked it."

"It's a lie."

"It's a white lie. Do what I tell you."

The boy grows up, goes to war, comes home and tells his best friend's family that their son's death in battle was so quick he never knew what had happened to him. A lie. The truth is their son died after six screaming hours of agony. Can such a lie be condemned? Is it conceivable that the soldier who came home safe had some moral duty to increase the pain and suffering of his friend's parents? Most would say that his lie was not only ethical but also, under the circumstances, necessary.

Let us go on. If the soldier's lie is excusable, what about the husband who lies to his wife about his one and only foolish love affair? And, if *his* lie is permissible, what about the one told by American president Bill Clinton about his affair with a Capitol Hill bimbo? It could be said that he did no more than follow the old code that gentlemen do not kiss and tell.

Few events so demonstrated the bending and breaking of principles as that well-publicized Clinton affair. The young woman involved was betrayed by a friend whom she trusted, not realizing the friend had a tape recorder and that her strongest sense of duty was to a political party, not to a friend. The same young woman was induced to testify by a repulsively righteous little man who gave her immunity in return for her evidence and who violated his own oath of office by leaking confidential material to the newspapers. Next came the editor of a pornographic magazine. He remarked that blow jobs were not new to the nation's capital. He offered a reward for information concerning other members of Congress and snared no less a figure than the Speaker of the House of Representatives, who had somehow forgotten his illicit affair until it became apparent that everybody else now knew and that he had no alternative to confession and resignation. His party people, the Republicans, wept real tears at the nobility he displayed by resigning at the same time they were trying to drive a Democratic Party president out of office for the identical offence.

This perhaps is the saddest thing about lying. It commonly brings out the worst qualities in everybody. This may be why we so dislike the word *liar*.

Few things are simple in this world, not even truth.

If that's illogical, well, I didn't promise you logic here. But that's a copout. So, to St. Pierres I will never see, this advice. When considering whether to lie, ask yourself one question and answer it to yourself with scrupulous honesty, or live with regrets. Ask yourself am I lying to help myself or lying to help people who deserve protection from truth? When honour requires you to tell a lie, construct one that looks like the truth.

In Trust We Trust

TO ST. PIERRES TOO FAR DOWN THE LINE for me to make out what they look like (I hope there'll be some blacks and Asians there), I say, "Trust your fellow man." I would go further and say trust even your rulers, but of course with sensible reservations because all governments lie, cheat and steal when they consider it necessary. Why do I say trust the people? Am I suggesting that the trusting soul is not betrayed by the clever and the wicked? Of course not. They get cheated. So do those who distrust everybody. No one is fireproofed against the world's trickery. For all that, it is better to be a trusting man.

There is a popular saying, "Treat every man as a friend and watch him for a rogue." It sounds all right but it leads to a narrow, crabbed, joyless existence and a timid, nervous passage through life. I am grateful I lived only on the fringes of poverty as a child. I had to wear my uncle's cast-off boots to school — they looked funny and I hated it — but in our house we always had food on the table and a dry warm bed at night. I was lucky to escape extreme poverty for the reason that it often exacts a heavy price later, even in times of prosperity. The extremely poor are apt to have a lifelong distrust of everybody, particularly other poor people. But let us speak of the ordinary man and woman.

Most people tend to be trusting. I've had time to observe many such people and learned something from it. I was never surprised when they were cheated. You could say that they asked for it. The surprising and instructive thing is that they were cheated so seldom. If there be a god who looks after drunks and fools, he perhaps also takes care of people who are too trusting of their fellow man. My conclusion, which has nothing to do with supernatural beings, is that the impulse of ordinary men and women is to act trustingly. They do so unthinkingly, perhaps, but they do it, obedient to a deep-rooted instinct to repay generosity and trust in the same coinage. The man who is more likely to be cheated is the soured soul who wasted his life sewing money into his underwear or poking it under the linoleum in the kitchen.

An old lawyer I knew, Fred Anderson, dead and buried these many decades, instructed me in business affairs once. Business was a study in which I never excelled, but I remember well his words about contracts.

"There are two ways to do a contract," he said. "One is to get the best lawyer in town to draw one up for you. Never the second best, only the best will do; even though he costs you more, he will cost you less. The other way is to have no papers at all and do the whole deal on a handshake. In my observation, one works just about as well as the other."

Old Fred, however, lived in an age when the captains of industry were the same men who came into the company as a floor sweeper at age 13. In our province, most business was face to face and handshake to handshake. Today's man has little such opportunity because enterprises are no longer the province of human beings but of corporations, and a corporation is, by definition, an organism that has no soul. This is why there are so many contracts written, with so much fine print, and they will continue to be written for the foreseeable future; they are attempts to bring honour and ethics into an organism that has no capacity to absorb such things.

The division of our world into fewer and fewer soulless giants and ever more individuals who have become more or less powerless has warped our capacity for trust. What, for instance, of theft? The taking of property that is not ours, you say? Oh, simple as that, you say?

Recently a man in Richmond, BC, a suburb of Vancouver, who had been saving money for his boy to start college, went to the banking machine and withdrew it all in cash, $5,000. Then he walked away and left the money in the tray. It happens. It's like the suburban housewife who comes home and shrieks, "My God,

I left the baby in the shopping cart!" He rushed back to the bank but he was too late. The money, unidentifiable in a way that cheques, credit cards and debit cards can never be, was gone beyond recall. Within an hour the woman who had picked up his money called him. She had traced him through the bank so she could give it back to him. When he tried to reward her and her husband they refused to take anything. East Indians, they were religious and said, "Give the reward money to God."

This was not a major news story in Greater Vancouver, nor should it have been. A man did not bite a dog. The people who found the money behaved as almost all of us feel we would have behaved, the way parents would tell children to behave, the way children would want to see their parents behave. Most people who kept money in those circumstances would have felt diminished.

But would we feel diminished if we stole in slightly altered circumstances? Consider another scenario. A government Liquor Control Board delivery truck, driving past your campsite on a country road, loses a keg of beer that rolls into the underbrush. The driver doesn't know he's lost the beer; he keeps driving off into the night. Neither does he return in the next hour, while you wait to see if he has discovered his loss. So you go to the nearest LCB store and tell them where they can find their missing keg of beer? LCB is not a human. It is a soulless organism. I would keep the beer. So would most people.

Different rules apply to matters between humans and humans and those between humans and institutions. Perhaps they shouldn't. They do.

As for the graceful act of trust, the sociologists can teach us something. Some of them recently enlisted computers to study altruism. Altruism is normally taken to mean giving up one's own goods, comfort or safety to help another person. The usual assumption is that we do this, and even the worst of us do it from time to time, because we may anticipate that others will do as much for us when it is our turn to need help. This is doubtless true. Ambrose Bierce expressed that idea with his usual cynicism when he said that gratitude is a lively sense of further favours to come. But what of the altruist who gives, and gives again, and then gives again, and it is never reciprocated? This was the sociologic question fed into the computer, which went its strange ways and came back with the answer that the unrewarded altruist was nevertheless better off than the more selfish individual. (The proof of this, like most things computers do, is beyond my comprehension but I believe it accurate as a matter of trust.)

Finally, for the readers who are not convinced, I add one more observation. People who are trusting seem to live longer and happier lives than other people. They are better company and, I suspect, their souls are shinier.

Intellectuals Have Meagre Souls

WHY DO WE SO OFTEN SUPPRESS SIMPLE TRUTHS, not only from other people, which is sneaky, but from ourselves, which can be damaging? A primal instinct may recognize a truth and we feel the urge to voice it, but almost all of us allow education or social pressure to submerge it, and usually only those of the lower social classes and a few drunks and poets let it out. So it is with our reverence for intellectuals. They deserve attention. They deserve no reverence.

I am indebted to John Ralston Saul, the brilliant author of *Voltaire's Bastards* and other works, for the insight I never attained myself—that intellectuals are untrustworthy and all too often have no souls. I should also have heeded Goethe, who, using the word *philosopher* instead of intellectual, wrote, "Give your philosopher everything. Give him wealth, give him gold, give him glory. But never give him power."

Scientists, who are often also intellectuals, have shown us that this thing called the soul, to which I so frequently refer, has no existence. Man has intelligence, instincts, memories, computing abilities, an understanding of spatial relationships and other similar qualities that, under the direction of genes and some chemicals, combine to form a personality. Intellectually I accept these many proofs that what we call our persona is what we used to call our soul. That acceptance, however, is only a construct of my intellect. In my heart I know I have a soul, and so do all the other people, and our souls know right from wrong. Poets could understand this as ordinary intellectuals could not: "The high soul seeks the high road, and the low soul gropes the low / and in between on the misty flats, the rest drift to and fro / but to every man there openeth, a high road and a low / and

243

every man decideth, the way his soul shall go." Intellect should be servant, not master.

From the most powerful of men to the most common, total reliance on intellect is the disease, not the cure. Robespierre was an intellectual, as were Torquemada and Himmler. So was Rousseau, who put all his many children into orphanages to die of starvation and neglect. The virtues of education, an intellectual pursuit, are clear enough and we all applaud it, or should. But it does not guarantee high moral values. It's worth noting that Germany's Waffen SS, which committed most of the battlefield atrocities in the Second World War, had a higher standard of education than the regular German army.

We may remind ourselves that Einstein was a quintessential intellectual, but let it also be noted that, to his credit, he never sought power and seemed rather to actively avoid it. Among the intellectuals who do seek power are some extremely dangerous men. There is nothing about brainpower or the capacity for philosophic thought that, of itself, guarantees that the individual has compassion, human understanding, loyalty, honour or any of the other forms human decency takes. He may have such qualities. Many do. Our peril is our tendency to make an automatic association of intellectual brilliance with nobility of soul. One bears no relationship to the other, any more than freckles relate to a taste for turnips.

Universities are natural nesting sites for intellectuals, and governments all over the world have gone to some trouble to preserve them against intrusion. Scholars need intellectual freedom and practically all the world's governments grant varying degrees of autonomy to universities so that vigorous and inquiring minds not be trammelled by the political and social conventions current at the moment. Within the institution the same thinking applies in the system called tenure. After serving an apprenticeship, a professor is given tenure and becomes almost unfireable, this to prevent him being dominated by intolerant, stupid or otherwise unsuitable presidents and chancellors. I am among many who would likely be prepared to light a pine faggot and march upon the wicked baron's castle if this protection of good minds were taken away. However, it would be easier to be enthusiastic if there were more evidence of free thought within universities.

Young people are by nature puritanical and intolerant. Having discovered, at about age 18, everything one needs to know, they insist that everybody else, their contemporaries and their elders, shall live up to their expectations. Alas, when an intolerant idea is in temporary ascendancy in a university the student body, often as not abetted by some of the professors, insist that only one truth is permissible and all others shall be shouted down. Visiting lecturers who nourish ideas found unpalatable are excluded from the campus, sometimes by rioting. There can be no crime more heinous than political incorrectness.

Some very bad ideas have thus been promoted by universities and a great many fresh, inquiring young minds bludgeoned into silent acquiescence. It is all too easy to forget that the students at old Heidelberg University were leaders in the mindless condemnation and persecution of the Jews, leading, not following Goebbels and the rest of the criminal ruling class of the day. I fully expect to see my first book-burning in Canada before I die and the promoters will almost surely be students while teaching staffs, those who haven't been locked out of their classrooms by sit-in strikers or fired on trumped-up sexism charges, will smile benignly and utter the usual humbug, proclaiming the bonfire to be evidence of concern for social justice. Bless and keep the universities but they are not the guardians of freedom; that is a role that can only be undertaken by individual men and women.

Intellectuals do help us to sort out many matters in our big, varied and often confusing world. They help excite our curiosity. They invite us to make more and better use of our own faculties. They often lead. Unfortunately the soulless among them lead us often into temptation and they seldom deliver us from evil.

How to Tell Sheepshit From Boston Baked Beans

Eric Hoffer, one of America's first and greatest philosophers, wrote a book, *The True Believer*, about such people. I have always known them in more common terms as the people who couldn't tell sheepshit from navy beans. By 2002 there were more of them than some people thought. They are the people who believe just about anything they are told. If told different things by different people, they resolve the matter by believing the last person who talked to them. They are curious folk who spend much of their lives waiting, as they say, for their ship to come in. They are seldom rich but are occasionally famous. In my observation, they tend to be happier than most people.

When one of their favourite ships of dreams is wrecked on the rocky reefs of reality they tend to be free of resentment against the pilot who steered them there. Almost immediately they find someone else who will guide them to instant health and wealth. They know they are going to be able to enjoy their good fortune almost indefinitely, because they drink Nubian goat milk and they have never seen a Nubian goat that had cancer. They are happy and, if confusion about sheepshit and beans doesn't bother them, perhaps it shouldn't bother the rest of us, unless they are cooking for us in a hunting camp.

However, it usually does bother us. We get tired of hearing them talk about it. How should those of us whose skepticism remains functional respond?

First, ask yourself whether *you* can tell shit from Shinola. In my seventies I did, and found that I frequently was not up to the task of selecting correctly. No man without a visceral belief in the Tooth Fairy would have bought some of the stocks I did. Some of the time we want to be fooled and if some snake oil salesman won't oblige us, we will fool ourselves. It has to do with a warping of the frontal lobe of the brain just over the left eyebrow, a theory of mine that I leave to the scientists for detailing. We all like to be fooled; it's just unfortunate that a few of us permit it to become an obsession.

Years ago, when schools were supplied with maps and even American schoolkids knew that Canada and Manchuria were in different places, I picked up a hitchhiker in the Fraser Canyon and took him as far as Hope, at the upper end of the Fraser Valley. He told me about his cousin, who had the farthest west farm in Canada, and provided me his name and address. I have no doubt whatever that he believed this; he just wanted to share the information with me. True believers are that way. Any newspaperman would have some interest in what he said. There had to be a small story there, a story about people who didn't know and didn't care, or a story about people who wrote of their uniqueness in cement on the barn floor or a story about people who had entered into correspondence with the farthest east farmer on the islands of Japan.

The farthest west farm stuck in my memory for months. One day, assigned to interview a visiting musician, I decided that if he really amounted to anything he would take an axe to his neighbour some day and we could pick him up in the ordinary way on the police blotter. Instead I started to drive to Tsawwassen to find our westernmost farm. I was an hour gone from the office before I consulted a map of memory, which had been in my head all along. Clearly there were farms on Vancouver Island, which was well west of the mouth of the Fraser. Beyond that, there were farms on the Queen Charlotte Islands, again farther to the westward. Although I didn't know it then, there was a farm at the junction of the Ogilvie and Yukon Rivers that was about halfway to Yokohama as longitude is measured. How could I have believed, even for an instant, in such patent nonsense? I believed, in part, because the man who told me was so obviously sincere but overwhelmingly because I wanted to, just as later, at considerably larger expense, I was to want to believe the stock promoter who arranged permission for me to put my gelt into the development of Moose Pasture Mines. It's a natural craving.

The prudent man, when he reaches 70, reminds himself more strongly that things that sound too good to be true almost always are, but he does not try to stamp out his residual faiths in Santa Claus, the Virgin of Guadalupe, goat milk, statistics or aloe vera, because whatever strange faiths are a part of his makeup cannot be eradicated, only sublimated. Our brains are flawed.

Joy

WHAT DOES MAN WANT FOR IN THIS WORLD? Very little. I can list my own wants on a single page.

> For me, it is fine woods, good leather, old silver and turquoise.
>
> Books.
>
> The smell of woodsmoke.
>
> The moan of a woman I am pleasuring.
>
> The dew of dawn and the evening star in the gloaming.
>
> Friendships.
>
> Azucena singing "Home to Our Mountains."
>
> Hunting dogs.
>
> Scrod, Boston baked beans, *chiles rellenos*, single malt Scotch, yellow-fat standing rib roasts, warm bread from the oven and Kahlua mixed with heavy cream.
>
> An eiderdown sleeping bag.
>
> Cool, clear water.
>
> A picked double on quail.
>
> Memories of old friends, old wine and old stories.
>
> New jokes.
>
> The mystery and magic of the English language.
>
> Love.

That's about it, for an entire lifetime. The computer says it's 123 words.

Conclusion

WE NEAR THE END OF THIS BOOK as I near the end of my life and find the great question unanswered. What was it all about? Why was I here? Whose purpose was served? John Bunyan's Pilgrim thought he knew these answers, so when he crossed over from life into death all the trumpets sounded for him on the other side. No trumpets will sound for me. I cannot summon up that comfortable belief in the supernatural. For me, death is a headlong plunge into an eternal nothing. If I could avoid it I would except perhaps that my children would not or could not avoid it, and there are few things sadder than children who die while parents live. But even as I write these words, I wonder if they are true. Would I really want to live forever, or even for a very long time?

I thank Daphne Bramham of the *Vancouver Sun* newspaper for thoughts read this very morning. (The best writing of the twentieth century has been newspaper writing, sometimes called the writing of history while it is happening. Intellectuals, who call it journalism, have always sneered at it. We in the trade, who always said that a journalist was a newspaperman who couldn't hold a job, knew that one of the surest proofs of the merit of our work was the contempt of the intellectuals and pseudo-intellectuals.)

Bramham notes that new stem cell research discoveries indicate that we may soon quite easily live beyond a hundred years. She then asks the question of whether we want to go much beyond the eighties. Our souls, she suggests, become weary by then. I am prompted to retract things said earlier in this book, suggesting I was going to hang around until people were really sick of seeing me.

As for this book, I am glad I wrote it. It gives me more personal satisfaction than any other I have written. There were times I even enjoyed writing it and that is far removed from the real world, because for me the writing of books has always been the exact opposite of the sexual act: the only enjoyment comes after it is over. This project was different.

To my descendants I say that if some of the time I spoke to you off the top of my head, there were others when I spoke from the depths of my heart.

As I wrote, I was changed and often puzzled. Time and again I found myself quoting the beliefs of organized religion. Most organized religious belief is to me nonsense, often dangerous nonsense, yet I am obliged to recognize that all those who pursue religions have one immense virtue: they know there is a question to be answered. They also often find truths. For this alone, society should respect them, lighten their taxes, as it does, hand them a few honours; just never let them have power.

Have I advice to give St. Pierres two, three or four generations hence? I have said no. Their world is bound to be very different from mine. By their time the fascist state, which I happen to dislike, may have withered and gone. Canadians may have regained their freedoms. Climate change may have blessed huge areas of this country while leaving much of the United States largely uninhabitable, with huge demographic and political changes resulting. On the other hand, terrorism may have turned us back to the age of the *condottieri*. Worse, nuclear blasts may have returned us to a condition where our main recreation is picking fleas off one another's backs.

Or science may have started us on a journey to the stars. Science, I am confident, will be as great a force for good as ever, although it suffers the fundamental flaw that it can tell us the how of almost everything but not the why.

I can speculate further about the future. I fancy that a century from today we shall be even more one world economically but simultaneously a multitude of nations culturally. Canada will have divided into English-speaking and French-speaking nations, to the benefit of both, and the same process will have reached the same logical conclusion in Spain, Britain and even in

251

that most intransigent of the unitary states, France. We will be unlikely to regret this fragmentation. The brotherly nations of Scandinavia showed us the way a century ago, with Swedes, Norwegians, Danes, Icelanders and Greenlanders all happier as friendly, culturally distinct states.

But all that is speculation, nothing more, and worth nothing much.

Memory will no doubt have played me false in this book, and there are any number of flaws. Despite all my words, I have failed to deal with love and humour, the two most important subjects. That is because I was unable to. Some things are too wonderful for me; there are some things I do not know: the way of an eagle in the air, the way of a ship upon the sea, the way of a serpent on the rock and the way of a man and a maid.

I hope these few truths have shone out of these chapters for those who follow me. Never underestimate the ordinary person's capacity for love, high principle, charity, self-sacrifice, courage and a general decency. The ordinary people are almost always of finer quality than their rulers. Take comfort from that fact. Do not expect to find much human decency in big governments, big corporations, big unions or any other large aggregations of humans in a hierarchic framework. Large organizations are, by definition, without souls. Like psychopaths, they can offer the charade of feeling pity, gratitude or other similar qualities we treasure in human beings but that is all it is, a masquerade. Do not blame them, any more than you would impute motives to an earthquake or a rainstorm; they are as incapable of wickedness as of goodness. It is futile for you to hunt for a heart in a stone. Try to use the giant organisms for good but for the most part find your own way to live without shame and die leaving the world a bit better than you found it. So go your own way.

Never underestimate the importance of what we call the arts. Neither underestimate your own ability to be an artist. In my own limited field of writing I have observed that almost every man and woman has at least one good story in them and I can believe the same applies to music, dance and all the rest. You will not learn to play basketball unless you pick up a ball and start bouncing it. Exercise your artistic talents, which you all possess in some degree.

Retreat from life from time to time. Be like Jesus Christ on the mountaintop or like the many aboriginal tribes whose youths retreated to wilderness, mortified the flesh and saw visions. We all need visions. They are hard to find in the noisy marketplace.

Riding this current of thought, learn to honour failure. It is the only key to progress. Wherever you are when you read these words, pause, look around you, observe your clothes, your timepiece, your communication machine, your spectacles or the colour on the walls of the room. Every single item is the product of failure after failure after failure. Finally, somebody built on the high hill of failure and heartbreak and made something work, but if he be wise he will honour the failures, both in other people and in himself, that carried him to success. Without mankind's constant refusal to accept failure as final we would still be sharing the last stinking remains of the lions' kill with the vultures and other carrion creatures. Failure is part of the fabric of life. If you have been pretty well free of failures, you aren't doing enough with your life; you should be risking more.

At the very least, risk having a generous heart. Mexico taught me a lot in the last half of the old century. It is a nation very different from ours, particularly because it is thousands of years older. I have watched the gringo tourists come and go. Those who expected song, dance, soft words and friendship found it everywhere. Those who expected to be cheated invariably were. That old country is one vast, ornately decorated mirror.

As we look at Mexico, we can look in the same way at the whole human race. We are capable of nobility but we are also from the nasty baboon side of the anthropoid family. I suppose it's a matter of a glass being half full or half empty. Most of my life I talked like a man who saw the glass half empty but the truth is, I knew it was half full. I was a pessimist but was confident that my pessimism was not justified.

    Goodbye, all you distant St. Pierres. I hope this book has been of some good to you. May you have love and money and the time for their enjoyment. May the wind be always at your back. May the good Lord hold you in the hollow of his hand.

Acknowledgements

My acknowledgements of the help of others in writing this book are beyond numbering or the power of memory to recall. Scores of wise men shared their wisdom with me over the decades, many so subtly I didn't know they were doing it. As for books, beyond the few I mention in the text and here, there were thousands more, read over seventy years, for I believe I learned something from every one of them except those I couldn't be bothered to finish. Yet for a book to list no acknowledgements is fraudulent. It suggests the writer was his own source for all knowledge. That is absurd. He picks all the brains he can find. Therefore, I shall try to acknowledge a few who helped me, even though my memory will fail to summon up most of them. Better some than none.

I owe an immense debt of gratitude to my editor, Naomi Pauls, who is smarter than I am but doesn't let it show. She has examined every word and sentence in this book; if there are errors, omissions, misquotations, false premises offered and wrong conclusions drawn, the fault is entirely hers. I just wanted to say it is a pleasure to work with someone like her.

Also my thanks to Pat Nagle, Sally McMahon, Marty Cox, Brenda Gillespie and other people I collared at random as testers. Some of them indicated that I had turned into a cranky old bastard, which reassured me that I was on the right track. I also mention my cousin, George Stanford, who contributes regularly to my enlightenment by providing lists of the current Darwin Awards, commemorating people whose improvement of the human gene pool consisted of dying instead of breeding.

There were newspaper and magazine articles beyond listing. For decades I have clipped them and filed them, and those yellowing papers now cascade out of dusty filing cabinets, usually with the essential material lost or, if found, with the source missing.

As for that multitude of books, a few rise above the mass like lighthouses on a crowded coastline, and I shall try to recall some of those authors: Aldous Huxley of *Brave New World*; Eric Blair (George Orwell) of *Animal Farm* and *1984*; Charles Lutwidge Dodgson (Lewis Carroll) of *Alice in Wonderland*; Francis Fukuyama of *Our Posthuman Future* and *The End of History and the Last Man*; Karl Marx, *Das Kapital*; Adam Smith, *Wealth of Nations*; Robert Townsend, *Up the Organization*; Don Marquis, *Archy and Mehitabel*; Joel Achenbach, *Why Things Are and Why Things Aren't*; Barbara Tuchman, *The Guns of August*; John J. Ratey, *A User's Guide to the Brain*; Dave McIntosh, *Ottawa Unbuttoned, or, Who's Running This Country Anyway?*; Joseph Heller, *Catch-22*... I'm running out of breath but want to name a few more: H.L. Mencken, Will Rogers, George Ade, Finley Peter Dunne, Russell Baker, Ambrose Bierce, Samuel Clemens (Mark Twain), R.T. "Colonel" Lowery, Winston Churchill, Lord Acton, Peter Newman, William F. Buckley, Hugh Trevor-Roper, Arnold Toynbee and nameless people at Eden Press, who tell you how to hide your money and yourself from your rulers. And just a few more: Joseph Conrad, Somerset Maugham, John Mortimer, John Le Carre, Len Deighton, Daniel Defoe, Robert Louis Stevenson, Sir Walter Scott, John Steinbeck and William Least Heat Moon. Although I never read her, I feel I was influenced by Barbara Cartland. Her only subject, a confection of romantic love, drenched with honey and covered with whipped cream, sold more books to more people than any other author, writing in any language, in all history. There is a message in Ms. Cartland's work.

Finally, for its poetry, beauty and knowledge of human nature, I am indebted to the Christian Bible, King James Version, the one printed before the dumbed down 1982 translation.